DATE DUE

Riverside Community Church
37W130 Crane Rd.
St. Charles, IL 60175
(630)443-7442

Six Battles Every Man Must Win

SIX
BATTLES
EVERY MAN
MUST WIN

...and the Ancient Secrets You'll Need to Succeed

BILL PERKINS

Tyndale House Publishers, Inc.
CAROL STREAM, ILLINOIS

Visit Tyndale's exciting Web site at www.tyndale.com.

TYNDALE and Tyndale's quill logo are registered trademarks of Tyndale House Publishers, Inc.

Six Battles Every Man Must Win

Designed by Ron Kaufmann

Edited by Karin Stock Buursma

Unless otherwise indicated, all Scripture quotations are taken from the *Holy Bible,* New International Version,® NIV.® Copyright © 1973, 1978, 1984 by Biblica, Inc.™ Used by permission of Zondervan. All rights reserved worldwide.

Scripture quotations marked NASB are taken from the *New American Standard Bible,* © 1960, 1962, 1963, 1968, 1971, 1972, 1973, 1975, 1977 by The Lockman Foundation. Used by permission.

Scripture quotations marked NLT are taken from the *Holy Bible,* New Living Translation, copyright © 1996. Used by permission of Tyndale House Publishers, Inc., Carol Stream, Illinois 60188. All rights reserved.

Scripture quotations marked *THE MESSAGE* are taken from *THE MESSAGE.* Copyright © 1993, 1994, 1995, 1996, 2000, 2001, 2002. Used by permission of NavPress Publishing Group.

Library of Congress Cataloging-in-Publication Data

Perkins, Bill, date.
   Six battles every man must win : and the ancient secrets you'll need to succeed / Bill Perkins.
     p. cm.
Includes bibliographical references.
   ISBN 978-0-8423-8287-8 (hc)
   1. Christian men—Religious life. 2. Bible. O.T. Samuel 2nd, XXIII—Criticism, interpretation, etc. I. Title.
BV4528.2.P47 2004
248.8'42—dc22   2003020549

Printed in the United States of America

15 14 13 12 11 10 09
13 12 11 10 9 8 7

*I dedicate this book to my favorite son. He has filled
my life with more joy than he can ever imagine.*

*Ryan—You were the first. I learned that I could love a child
more than life. And I do. You've always been my favorite.
I wrestled with you first, played soccer with you first,
memorized Scripture with you first, and loved you first. You're
my favorite. And I know God will use you to touch the world.*

❦

*David—With you I learned that no two kids are alike.
I discovered that creativity and fun are endless. And you
are my favorite—even though you find it hard to believe,
it's true. Yes, I tell the others this. But David, I love you
the most. Your friendship will change the world.*

❦

*Paul—I learned that a son can be more mature than his dad
and a better leader. As you've always known—you're my
favorite. I realize you believe this. And you should since it's
true. Please, keep it between us. Don't tell your brothers.
I know your faithfulness will change the world.*

CONTENTS

ACKNOWLEDGMENTS

Before the music starts,
I'd like you to meet the band.

. . .

Editors extraordinaire:
Karin Buursma, Lisa Jackson, and Barbara Kois,
without whom the flat notes would remain.

. . .

John Van Diest: my friend and the man who believed
this message should be heard.

. . .

The unnamed men and women who teamed up with
Tyndale to read the initial draft of the book. Their
insights helped strengthen the weak places. . . .

CHAPTER ONE

LIVE AS THOUGH NOTHING *ELSE* MATTERS

As a child living in New Mexico, I remember looking up at the star-stenciled night sky and thinking, "Someone created all of this, and I want to know him. I want to be on his side."

But I didn't know God, and I had no idea how to meet him. Equally troublesome was the fact that my life had no direction. I was only a kid, but I sensed that knowing God would give my life meaning.

Years later, when I met God, he did just that. But like a lot of men, I tend to lose my spiritual focus. I forget the radical changes God brought to my life, and I find it easy to get trapped in an eddy of spiritual passivity. Round and round I go with lots of activity but no direction. At such times I realize I'm living with the same purposelessness I knew as a boy.

Do you know what I mean? If so, you're probably as

concerned with your bent toward spiritual passivity as I am with mine. This book was written for men who, like me, are tired of living like spiritual weaklings. It's for men who believe they were created to be warriors but aren't sure how to fight or what they should be fighting for. It's for men who want to lock onto their purpose for living. And it's for men who want to learn ancient secrets from some of the greatest warriors of the Bible: David's special fighting force, the mighty men.

> Like a lot of men, I tend to lose my spiritual focus. I forget the radical changes God brought to my life, and I find it easy to get trapped in an eddy of spiritual passivity.

But wait a minute. I'm getting ahead of myself and need to get back to the story of how I met God. Like I said, as a kid I wanted to know God but didn't know how. One day I asked a friend what I had to do to know God and he said, "It's simple, really. God is in heaven holding a giant scale. On the left side he places your good deeds and on the right side your bad ones. As long as your good deeds outweigh your bad deeds, you're in with God."

While such a religious philosophy may have seemed simple to him, it didn't help me at all. The more I evaluated my "deeds," the more I realized the scale wasn't tipping in the right direction.

I had another friend who attended church every Sunday. I asked him the same question. He told me I needed to be baptized. He explained that the water of baptism miraculously had the power to wash away the guilt of my past sins.

"And what about those I commit in the future?" I asked.

"Well, just don't sin after you're baptized and you'll be okay," he said. "Besides, once you're baptized, you won't want to sin."

I was ten at the time and decided to wait until I was twelve to take the big plunge. As unbelievable as it sounds, I thought that by age twelve I would be through sinning. I looked at adults and naively believed they didn't do bad things—at least not as many as I did.

The church I visited with my friend usually baptized by sprinkling, but once a year they baptized by immersion. I figured the sprinkling was for people who hadn't sinned much, so I decided to be immersed. I still remember getting out of the water and thinking, *All I have to do now is never sin again.* I even managed to make it for several seconds without sinning. However, less than an hour after the momentous event I realized the baptism must not have "taken." Nothing within me had changed. I felt and acted exactly the same as I had before.

I told my friend that baptism didn't seem to have had an effect on me. That's when he informed me that baptism is like a base hit: It gets a person to first base but it doesn't guarantee he'll make it home.

"So what else do I have to do?" I asked.

"Just do the best you can," he said. "God grades on a curve."

Something about that last statement made me uncomfortable, probably because I was a terrible student. I remember taking a health class in which we had to name every bone in the human body. I managed to name them

all—funny bone, neck bone, collarbone, pinky, index finger, knee bone, big toe, and so on.

A few days later I asked the teacher, "Are you going to grade on a curve?"

He smiled, and I felt a momentary rush of relief. Then he said, "Perkins, I could curve the test fifty points and you'd still flunk." The next day I got the test back and saw a great big nine written on it in red ink. I immediately thought about God. What if I only score a nine on my life morality test? I'm doomed.

> **We must daily remind ourselves that compared to knowing God and fighting at his side, nothing *else* matters.**

It was at that moment I concluded that although God exists, he could no more be known than fictional characters like Santa Claus or Superman. And if God couldn't be known, then life was a maze with no purpose except to get through it—and getting through it unscathed proved impossible for me.

It wasn't until I was a freshman at the University of Texas that a meltdown with three crucial people drove me to God. Within a month I had destroyed my relationship with my girlfriend, my best friend, and my mentor. I had repeatedly and deeply hurt the people I loved the most. The painful realization that I was the world's greatest jerk and had destroyed my best hopes for love and friendship drove me into a deep depression. Unable to do anything more than nibble at my food, I saw my weight drop from 145 pounds to 130 pounds. I looked and felt like a walking dead man.

During the darkest moment of my depression, I knelt beside my bed and cried out to God, "I don't know if you can hear me, but if you can, please save me from myself."

I didn't expect anything to happen and it didn't—at least not right away. A few weeks later I met a student on campus, and he asked me if anyone had ever shown me from the Bible how I could know God. That seemed like a novel approach.

I had already learned that I could no more earn God's favor than I could jump to the moon, so the concept of Jesus dying in my place to take the punishment for all my sins made sense to me. So did the idea that God would accept me on the basis of faith and not baptism or good works. Over the next several months, as my understanding grew, I entered into a relationship with God. And I celebrated the fact that he welcomed my friendship.

Immediately I saw significant changes in my life. Since childhood I had tried to stop cussing and never succeeded. God replaced the cesspool in my soul with a spring of fresh water, and it affected my speech.

I had committed many sins in my nineteen or so years of life. When I looked at the Ten Commandments I knew for sure that the only one I hadn't committed was murder. Yet I had found forgiveness. Words can't capture the feelings of a forgiven man. I felt clean, and it was wonderful.

I also lived with a new sense of wonder. The change proved as extreme as turning on a light in a dark room and exposing a treasure that had been there all along.

But the most radical change involved the way I viewed

life. I realized that nothing else mattered when compared to knowing God. Not money, power, fame, sex, or even family.

Once I allowed this reality to govern my life, everything else took on meaning. I had found the box top to a puzzle, or it had found me, and the pieces now had a place. I became a young man with a mission and a purpose. I wanted to know God better, and I wanted to help others know him. God became my ballast and my compass, keeping me upright and headed in the right direction.

We must cast aside our passivity and live as the warriors God created us to be.

That experience changed what I believe and changed the course of my life. What disturbs me is that now, years later, while I still believe that nothing *else* matters compared to knowing God, I often live as though I don't believe it. I struggle with spiritual passivity. It eats away at me as covertly as termites in the walls of my house. And I know that most men are weakened in the same way.

How can we combat this passivity? We must choose to live with a focus on God. We must daily remind ourselves that compared to knowing him and fighting at his side, nothing else matters. We must live as the warriors God created us to be. As you'll see in the remainder of this book, God equipped us to win the six biggest battles of a man's life.

Winning these battles begins with an understanding of the broader war of which each battle is a part. In the next chapter you'll discover that we're all involved in the great

angelic conflict, which is a spiritual war for the hearts of men. Yes, angels, both fallen and unfallen, are involved in this war, and your heart is the battleground.

Discussion Questions

1. On your own spiritual journey, what kinds of things have you thought would bring you into a relationship with God?

2. Suppose you were to stand before God and he asked you, "Why should I let you into heaven?" What would you tell him?

3. Take a moment to read Romans 4:5, Ephesians 2:8-9, and John 3:18. Can you identify what the Bible says about why God should let you into heaven? Do you feel you've met that qualification? Why or why not?

4. Can you say that compared to knowing God and fighting at his side, nothing else matters?

5. If you lived as though nothing else mattered compared to knowing God and fighting at his side, what would your life look like?

If you would like to trust Jesus Christ, you can do so now with a simple prayer of faith:

"Father, I believe Jesus died on the cross to pay for my sins. I believe he was raised from the dead.

I would now like to trust him alone for forgiveness and eternal life. Amen."

If you prayed that prayer and put your faith in Christ, the Bible promises you have forgiveness and eternal life (John 3:16).

THE GREAT ANGELIC CONFLICT

I'm not sure who dreams up such bizarre experiments, but one performed by the National Institute of Mental Health illustrates what sometimes happens to Christian men in our society.

The experiment took place in a nine-foot-square cage designed to comfortably house 160 mice. In two and a half years, the colony of mice grew from 8 to 2,200. Yes, you read that right. While I'm not sure how the researchers counted them, some 2,200 mice all lived in one cage.

As the population grew, research psychologist Dr. John Calhoun began to observe changes in the mice's behavior. Eventually, the mouse society started to fall apart. Here's what Dr. Calhoun reported:

- Adults formed groups or cliques of about a dozen mice per group.
- The males who normally protected their territory withdrew from leadership and became uncharacteristically passive.
- The females became unusually aggressive and forced out the young.
- The whole "mouse society" became disrupted. And after five years *all the mice had died* even though there was an abundance of food, water, and resources, and an absence of disease.[1]

While we're not mice, we do live in an increasingly crowded and impersonal world. In some respects we behave like that mouse society. As men we've become disconnected and isolated. Many of us don't have a single friend with whom we can share our joys and struggles. Most distressing is the passivity of Christian men. We no longer defend our territory. We refuse to fight for what's important—or at least what is important to God. We seldom live as though nothing else matters compared to knowing God. Indeed, we live as though everything else matters. And in the process, we lose the battles we must win.

How has this happened? Although multiple elements have shaped our thinking, I'm convinced that one significant factor is that for decades the secular culture has told men to cultivate their gentler side.* And in the process, this way of

---

*In the next chapter I'll discuss how the Christian culture has feminized men.

thinking has begun to shape our identity. A few prominent writers have actually exhorted men to—get this—"tap into their feminine side." I can hardly write the words without getting finger cramps.

Now, don't get me wrong. We all need to cultivate sensitivity and strengthen our communication skills. But we don't need to become women to do that.

I reject the idea that it's somehow a bad thing to be a man. By "man" I don't just mean male instead of female. By "man" I mean physically strong, emotionally tough, and mentally and spiritually combative. I'm speaking of men who enjoy football, rugby, hockey, hoops, NASCAR, golf, and war movies. I'm talking about men who work as firefighters, marines, and police officers and thrive on competition and adventure. I'm referring to men who enjoy chess, cards, and a three-hour tennis match.

> **As men we've become disconnected and isolated.... We no longer defend our territory.**

If you're reading thoughtfully, that last sentence may have captured your attention like a zebra in a herd of white stallions. Yes, I said men who enjoy chess, cards, and tennis. This isn't an issue of personality or recreational preference. It's about being a man. Regardless of a man's personality, at his core he enjoys the excitement of a battle and the pleasure of victory.

SPIRITUAL COMBATANTS

You see, I'm convinced God created men to be harder than rocks. God told Adam, the first man, to "subdue" the earth

and "rule over" all the creatures on land, in the air, and in the sea (Genesis 1:28).[2] Obedience to such a command would require a man to be as hard as nails and to be driven by a spiritual power strong enough to drive spikes through stone.

> God has placed us in the middle of an angelic war between his angels of light and Satan's demons of darkness.

But that's only part of the story because it involves man's role in the physical world—the part we can see, hear, taste, touch, and smell. We aren't just bodies and minds; we're spiritual beings. In the spiritual dimension, God has placed us in the middle of an angelic war between his angels of light and Satan's demons of darkness (Ephesians 6:12).

While our enemy may be invisible, he isn't powerless. Peter compares Satan to a roaring lion seeking someone to devour (1 Peter 5:8), while Paul warns us that Satan deceives us by masquerading as an angel of light (2 Corinthians 11:14). Throughout his ministry Jesus openly confronted demons who served their evil master by inflicting people with mental illness and physical disabilities.

THE GREAT ANGELIC CONFLICT

Every dark and evil character created to evoke fear in readers and moviegoers is only the devil's shadow. No battle scene from The Lord of the Rings compares with the ferocity of the angelic conflict. Even the dreaded Borg, of *Star Trek* infamy, are assimilated by the devil and his army of demons. The masses slaughtered by Hitler and Stalin represent only a fraction of the lives destroyed by Satan.

Throughout the Bible men are urged to fight the enemy, do battle, and wage war. We've not been placed in a spiritual Disneyland and told to "have fun." At birth we entered a battlefield. At the time of our rebirth in Christ we enlisted in God's army as warriors of light.

Abraham's nephew Lot learned this lesson on the evening the two angels told him to gather his family and get out of town because God intended to destroy the city of Sodom. High on a mountain Moses realized he was involved in a spiritual battle when the angel of the Lord appeared to him in the flames of a burning bush. He informed Moses that he had just been recruited to take on Pharaoh and release the Hebrew slaves. Gideon lacked spiritual vision until the day the angel of the Lord interrupted his life and sent him to battle the Midianites—idolatrous people who were oppressing the Israelites. The stories could go on and on. Each of these men, and others, fought in the power of their God against forces empowered by Satan and his demons.

Today the conflict is spiritual and the war is for our heart—the core of our being that serves as the center of our intellect, emotions, and will.

Today the conflict is spiritual and the war is for our heart—the core of our being that serves as the center of our intellect, emotion, and will. The enemy wants to capture our affection and direct our plans. He seeks to destroy us and our family. If we lose this war, not only is strategic ground lost, but even worse, we align ourselves with the enemy.

No weapon of the enemy has been more effective than the barrage of propaganda that hammers away at our thinking and convinces us we're not warriors. It urges us to kick back and watch the world pass by like a parade. Such passivity reeks of danger. It's a vampire that sinks its fangs into our neck and subtly redirects our loyalty to the dark side. It sucks out our spiritual lifeblood so we're drained of God's power.

We must wake up. We can no longer deny the reality of the angelic conflict in which we're combatants. We have an enemy who hates us and seeks our destruction. As God's warriors we must live as though nothing *else* matters compared with knowing him and fighting at his side. We must discover the secret of masculine strength that's rooted in Christ.

Perhaps you can't see yourself fighting in the spiritual arena because you don't *feel* driven to battle the forces of hell. But the God who created you placed a desire for battle in your heart, and he intends to harness that desire and use it for his kingdom.

CHILDHOOD DREAMS

If we pause and reflect on our own motivation, we see that it's the warrior within that drives us, for good or for bad. This inner warrior drives us to excel, to beat the competition, and to get the most "stuff." Think about your childhood fantasies. When you imagined playing professional baseball or football, did you ever dream of striking out in the bottom of the ninth inning and losing the final

game of the World Series? Did you ever imagine throwing an interception during the Super Bowl? Of course not! As a boy you probably dreamed of hitting a game-winning home run or scoring a touchdown in the final seconds of a championship game. Why? Because God placed within us all a yearning for victory. This is the essence of our manhood.

In our childhood dreams, we fight like our heroes—Superman, Spider-Man, and other powerful men—who defeated the forces of evil against great odds. And then we encounter reality. We learn that life is tough. As Patrick Morley once said, "Life's not a bowling game in which we're the ball. If anything, we're a pin, and life is the bowling ball that keeps knocking us down."

Eventually, we grow up and the disappointment that comes from being repeatedly knocked down causes us to view our earlier dreams of heroic victory as childish. We no longer think of ourselves as conquering heroes. Instead of cultivating the masculine strength God has given us to wage spiritual war, we squeeze the warrior within, making him tiny—like a compressed foam ball. Our identity rests in failure and disappointment instead of in God.

While a part of us craves combat and victory, we've believed the culture's lie that says we're spectators, not warriors. Rather than fighting in the real war, we engage in vicarious battles from the seat of a theatre or on the sideline of a football game. God's army of believing men has become a toothless and clawless tiger interested only in being entertained.

WHY IS LIFE SO HARD?

The repeated blows of life break the hardest man. Yet God allows you to get knocked down by hardship, discourage-ment, and even defeat as a means of toughening you up for a bigger battle. The evil one wants you to see yourself as a civilian, but you must ignore his direction and live like a conquering warrior.

A lot of men have told me this message resonates with them—so I hope it connects with you, too. I'm sure some-thing within you cries to slip on the armor and enter the fray. That's because God created you to be a warrior, lock-ing arms with other men, storming the gates of hell.

The disappointments of life aren't intended to strip away your manhood. God allowed every hardship you've experienced to strengthen you by driving you to him. Once you tap into his power and unleash the warrior within, you'll win the most ferocious battles. You'll fight like the mighty men of old.

DAVID'S MIGHTY MEN

Recently I went through a time when despair squeezed my soul like a massive boa constrictor. I had poured eleven years into a vision that never materialized. Everything I did to create momentum collapsed like a deflated balloon. Without a financial parachute or an offer of employment elsewhere, God prompted me to walk away.

"And do what?" my wife asked.

I gazed at her for several moments and then whispered softly, "I don't know."

Such "failure" struck at the heart of my self-worth. In those months, I didn't feel like a conquering warrior. I felt like hardship had touched me and somehow caused me to get smaller—to shrink. I felt beaten and discouraged. Uncertain about the future, I opened my Bible, wanting to find something that would pry loose the constrictor and give me a breath of hope.

I realized the mighty men of David hadn't always been mighty.... How had they been transformed from losers to "mighty" men?

At the end of the Old Testament book of 2 Samuel, I found King David's last words. Of course, I already knew about his many heroic feats—defeating Goliath, beating the Philistines, and expanding Israel's territory. I realized he hadn't conquered his enemies alone any more than a championship team wins because of one superstar. Seeking to underline this truth, the author of 2 Samuel described a band of men whose faith and courage, like wind under the wings of an eagle, lifted David over his enemies and placed him on the throne.

He wrote, "These are the names of David's mighty men" (2 Samuel 23:8). That eight-word sentence grabbed my attention and I sat up in my chair. I quickly read the remainder of the chapter and was blown away by the heroic feats of three of these mighty men—including winning battles against overwhelming odds. *Who are these guys?* I wondered. They sounded like an ancient version of real-life superheroes.

I had read the story before but had given it no more attention than a footnote. When I looked at David's life

again, it struck me that there was a long gap between when the prophet Samuel anointed David as Israel's next king and when he actually took the throne. Following David's defeat of Goliath, King Saul envied David's popularity and tried to kill David. Eventually he chased David into the wilderness, where he spent several years on the run. It was here that David began to gather followers—some of whom became the mighty men.

I could identify with David's early success followed by a series of disappointments. I also knew how it felt to suffer betrayal from a friend. Yet I've never suffered like David. I had a bed to sleep on and a roof to sleep under. David had neither. For years the king's army hunted for the giant-killer turned fugitive. Like a spider in a crack, David found refuge in caves and canyons and anywhere else he could hide.

In spite of—or maybe because of—his hardships, I knew David had attracted an army of broken men, so I turned to that part of the story. Here's what I found: "All those who were in distress or in debt or discontented gathered around him, and he became their leader" (I Samuel 22:2).

The instant I read that sentence my eyes opened wide. I realized the mighty men of David hadn't always been mighty. For whatever reason, they hadn't succeeded in King Saul's army . . . or other facets of life, for that matter. They knew the pain of unpaid bills, shattered friendships, and public scorn. Like beggars living under a bridge, they seemed unlikely candidates for greatness.

How had they been transformed from losers to mighty men? The common thread among these men was that they

rallied around the man God had designated as the future king, and in doing so, identified with God's purpose. They stepped into the angelic conflict on God's side and fought in his power. This meant they had to take a stand against the evil plans of King Saul and fight against the Philistines and Moabites—idolatrous nations who rejected the God of Israel and mocked his strength. At some point in time each of these men fought with valor and proved they deserved the title "mighty men."

As I reflected on these warriors I felt God's presence— as though glowing embers in my soul had been stoked by a soft breath from God. The words inflamed my spirit. I reminded myself that I too am involved in the great angelic conflict and that God will enable me to fight victoriously in the battle against hell for the hearts of men.

But I wanted to learn more about these beggars turned knights, so I dug deeper into the text, hoping to unearth more gold. What I found didn't disappoint me. I saw that to become mighty men, these warriors had to fight six battles: for their identity, for personal holiness, for their family, for endurance through pain, for their friends, and for a strong faith. Those six battles are still the same for us today. As you read the following chapter, you'll gain insight into what you must do before you can win the six crucial battles in which you're engaged.

Discussion Questions

1. Why do boys often dream of becoming conquering warriors? What were your childhood dreams like?

2. What is the "great angelic conflict"? How do our childhood dreams prepare us for spiritual conflict?

3. How does life try to convince us we're not warriors?

4. What were David's mighty men like before they met him (1 Samuel 22:2)?

5. Can you identify with David's mighty men as they are described in 1 Samuel 22:2? Does it give you hope to know about their background? Why or why not?

STAND YOUR GROUND

Winning the War for Your Heart

When I was a boy my dad once told me, "Never start a fight, son. But if you have no other option, hit first, hit fast, and hit hard." I had all but forgotten his words until one night when my six-year-old son, a saddle of freckles on his nose, told me two classmates were throwing rocks at him while they walked to school every morning.

After swallowing my anger and deciding to withhold my dad's advice, I looked Ryan in the eyes and said, "Tell them to stop."

"I did," he said. "They just laughed and picked up another rock."

"Ask your mother to tell them to stop," I said.

"I did."

"And?"

"Come on, Dad. What do you think happened?"

"They ignored her."

"Right."

Naively believing all fathers had the wit of Bill Cosby and the wisdom of Ben Cartwright, I told Ryan I'd call the father of one of the boys. A few minutes later I picked up the phone and called Walt, a bear of a man I had met at a boring back-to-school night. He seemed nice enough and I assumed he would want to work out a peaceful solution.

Even Jesus fought to defend what he valued.

"Walt, your boy has been throwing rocks at Ryan during their morning walk to school. I was hoping you'd ask him to throw them in a different direction."

After a moment of silence, Walt cleared his throat and said, "You know, Bill, when I was a boy my dad always told me to work out these things myself. Why don't we just let the boys work it out?"

I quickly surmised Walt had graduated from the Homer Simpson school of parenting and didn't believe in parental intervention.

"Yeah, my dad used to tell me something like that too," I said. I figured I wouldn't mention the specifics of my dad's advice. The bear-man might not like my dad's approach to conflict resolution. "That sounds like a plan to me," I added.

I hung up the phone and returned to Ryan's room and told him, "I spoke with Joe's dad."

"What did he say?"

In that moment I had to make an important decision. It

took me about a half a second. "He said if his son picks up a rock tomorrow, you're to hit first, fast, and hard."

Ryan cocked his head to one side and with a look of disbelief said, "You're kidding. Right?"

"Yeah, I'm kidding. But that's what I want you to do."

Occasionally, someone will ask me how I could give such advice in light of Jesus' command to turn our other cheek when we're hit (Matthew 5:39). I don't believe Jesus told us not to defend ourselves. I think he was teaching us not to allow someone else to control our behavior. If I'm hit and retaliate in kind, the person who hit me has control over my behavior. Jesus wanted his followers to submit to him, not to their passions or the threats of an enemy. But as we'll see later, even Jesus fought to defend what he valued.

Anyway, Ryan wasn't concerned about such questions and I knew he had to defend himself. The next day I felt like a trainer waiting for the judge's decision at the end of a twelve-round fight. I left work early to meet Ryan when he got home from school. At 2:30 he walked through the front door with a smiling face, all of his teeth, all of his freckles, and no bruises or broken bones.

"I did exactly what you told me to do," Ryan said. "Joe started to pick up a rock and I hit him. He started crying and said, 'I'm going to tell your dad.' "

Ryan paused. "I said, 'Go ahead. He put me up to it!' "

"What happened next?" I asked.

"He stopped crying and we walked to school."

I tell that story because I'm convinced most fathers

would urge a son or daughter to stand up to a bully. They know that kids who don't defend themselves run the risk of being treated like a cat by the campus dogs. While some dads may suggest a different course of action and perhaps a less aggressive one, they would still advise a gutsy response.

A GENERATION OF GEORGE McFLYS

What's disturbing is that many men refuse to take the same advice they would offer to their own sons and daughters. We refuse to stand up to the intimidating bullies of our culture. Consequently, we live in a time of spiritually passive men who can't see that they've become spiritual jellyfish flowing with the cultural currents.

We've become a generation of George McFlys—weak-willed men like Marty's dad in *Back to the Future*. If you've seen the movie you probably recall how Biff Tannen, a teenager with a barrel for a neck and oaks for arms, repeatedly bullies and humiliates George, much to the shame and embarrassment of his son.

Like pathetic, chicken-chested George, we smile, nod our heads, and do what Biff demands.

How did this happen? In addition to the propaganda of the culture, the church has played a major role in the emasculation of Christian men. The process has occurred slowly over more than a century.

During the Industrial Revolution, men left the close-knit setting of their family to work in the factory and pursue the materialistic benefits that flowed from an increased income.

Left at home to care for the children, women became the spiritual leaders of the family, taking the kids to church and nurturing their faith. Men stopped debating theology in the church and pursued business and recreation. They handed off the education of their children to public schools and Sunday school, where the teachers were primarily women.

Many men refuse to take the same advice they would offer their own sons and daughters.

As fewer men attended church, women assumed roles of teaching and leadership that had once been occupied by men. This continues today. According to research conducted by the Barna Research Group, women are twice as likely as men to be involved in discipleship at a church, 57 percent more likely to attend Sunday school, 56 percent more likely to hold a leadership position, and 54 percent more likely to participate in a small group.[1]

In light of the above data, I think churches created a more feminine setting to meet the needs of the growing female population. If you question the validity of such a conclusion, call your church and ask how much money is budgeted separately for women's and men's ministries. If you attend a multistaffed church you may be surprised by the inequity of spending.

It's probably no surprise that many church buildings were designed and decorated with women in mind. Consider the different settings in which men and women thrive.

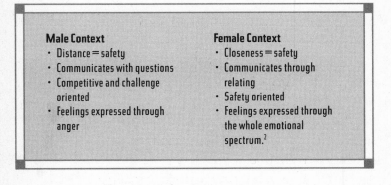

Male Context
- Distance = safety
- Communicates with questions
- Competitive and challenge oriented
- Feelings expressed through anger

Female Context
- Closeness = safety
- Communicates through relating
- Safety oriented
- Feelings expressed through the whole emotional spectrum.[2]

If you think about a typical church setting, does it encourage physical distance or closeness? Is the greater emphasis on building relationships or asking tough questions? Does it encourage competition and extend a challenge, or does it shy away from competition? Does it encourage a healthy expression of anger or see most expressions of anger as sinful?

If you answered most of those questions as I would, it's apparent that many churches are built to provide a safe environment for women.* In the process they prove as comfortable for many men as a meeting of the La Leche League.

Men frequent places where they can be themselves without holding back or fearing rejection. Places like football stadiums, basketball and hockey arenas, golf courses, car racetracks, fishing holes, and pubs. If you ask most men if they think of church as a place where they have to hold

---

*I don't mean to imply that all churches create a feminine setting. There are numerous pastors and church leaders who have realized the need to create an environment that appeals to men and have done so. Most of them have been rewarded with dynamic and growing churches with strong male involvement.

back, I suspect the vast majority would answer with an emphatic yes.

Recognizing the need to care for women, pastors adapted their messages with their primary audience in mind. One outcome of this is that for decades pastors have painted a picture of gentle Jesus, with baby-soft hands and a chalky face, and urged us to follow his lead. At the same time church leaders created an environment as inviting for men as a women's hair salon.

Certainly Jesus expressed compassion and gentleness. But that's only part of the story. How about when he cleared the temple of the dishonest money changers who ripped off the people in the name of religion? I see a man with fire in his eyes. I see strong, calloused hands wildly waving leather straps and muscular arms overturning heavy tables, dumping out money, and chasing sheep, cattle, and money changers out of the temple (John 2:13-16). Gentle Jesus? Hardly.

Certainly Jesus expressed compassion and gentleness. But that's only part of the story.

I'm sure the ancient religious leaders didn't appreciate the gentle side of Jesus the day he stood before a crowd of regulars, pointed a finger in the face of the self-righteous leaders, and used his words to rip off their religious mask and expose the monster hiding behind it. He called them a pack of "hypocrites," "blind guides," and "fools" (Matthew 23:13-36).

Are men urged to follow this example? No way! Instead of encouraging men to tap into their God-given strength

and express it appropriately, the church has sought to feminize them.

I'm not suggesting Christian men should publicly rebuke leaders. Rather, I think we need to follow Jesus' example in aggressively pursuing God and fighting against evil in the battle for the heart.

Since the church has failed to show men godly masculinity through Jesus' example, it's no surprise they are ill-equipped to resist the cultural misconceptions of manliness. While numerous cultural viewpoints seek to control men, there are two in particular that dominate men like the big bad wolf.

CULTURAL BULLY #1:
YOU ARE WHAT YOU OWN

Every morning millions of men climb out of bed, shower, shave, and don their "uniforms"—which signify both their rank and branch of service—and hit the road for work. They battle traffic, fatigue, stress, burnout, and the competition.

When asked why they work so long and hard, most men will admit they're just trying to get ahead. If asked, "Ahead of what?" they usually say either, "The bills," or "Ahead—you know—ahead of where I am now."

Men are driven to win the marketplace war because of the tangible spoils of victory. The winners are easily spotted by their lakeside homes, Mercedes, ski boats, European vacations, corner offices, and of course the powerful people they know—or better yet, the powerful people who know them.

Nobody ever said a war could be won without a few casualties. If a man has to sacrifice his family and health—so what? Of course, when he suffers from a heart attack or his wife walks out the door with the kids in tow, swearing never to return, he wonders if maybe the price wasn't a bit too high. But by then he's trapped in the battle, like a marine pinned down in a trench during a firefight, and he feels he can't get out. He's got a mortgage, two car payments, and a boat payment, not to mention the monthly credit card balance. The emotional and physical toll creates a deep and lingering pain.

Instead of realizing that he's fighting in the wrong war, the man redoubles his efforts and works that much harder. *Weekend warrior* is a term that applies not only to men who recreate on weekends but also to men who have a second job on weekends.[3] All of this because our culture tells us the measure of a man's worth is what he owns.

While he may win the war for financial success, the wounds run deep. Even if a man manages to make big bucks and occupy a position of influence, the ache in his heart persists. He agonizes because what he thought would bring lasting gratification only increases his need for more. His hunger, like an elastic bag, is never filled—it just expands. All he's worked so hard to achieve cannot fill his heart.

If he fails to win the battle and works for minimum wage, lives in a small home or apartment, and drives a used car or rides a bus, his pain—part grief and part self-loathing—eats away at his self-respect.

It's no wonder so many men search for something to deaden the pain of their battle wounds. And increasingly men are looking in the same place.

CULTURAL BULLY #2:
MEDICATE YOUR PAIN WITH SEX

During a two-month period I talked with more than four hundred men, trying to understand their core needs and heartfelt struggles. It didn't take long for me to discover that most of them suffered from battle fatigue.

Prior to this I had conducted extensive surveys in churches to discover the areas where men struggle the most. I wasn't surprised to learn that more than 55 percent indicated their biggest moral battle involved sexual purity.

> **More than 55 percent of surveyed men indicated their biggest moral battle involved sexual purity.**

Not that long ago men had to slither into a dirty building with blacked-out windows on the seedy side of town to view sexually explicit films. Today erotica is as easy to access as the click of a mouse or the push of a button on a television remote control. Christian men can watch whatever they want without the fear of being discovered.

And the odds of a payout are greater than at any casino in Las Vegas. Like a gambler who has to increase the size of his bet to get a rush, a man can increase the release of adrenaline and endorphins into his body by viewing ever more explicit images.

Satan delights in taking something good and distorting

it for evil ends. His battle plan is simple: capture a man's soul with illicit sex. He doesn't want your car, home, boat, job, clothes, status, or health. He wants your heart. And he knows how to capture it.

Like the song of the ancient sirens, the images of beautiful women lure men into the world of pornography. Every day more men log on to the Internet in search of a sexual rush.

Writing for the *New York Times,* Timothy Egan commented on the growth of the porn industry: "The business of selling sexual desire through images has become a $10 billion annual industry in the United States, according to the Forrester Research of Cambridge, Massachusetts, and the industry's own Securities and Exchange Commission filing."[4] By the time this book is in print that number will no doubt be even higher.

If we're going to fulfill our God-given purpose as men, it's imperative that we stand up to these cultural bullies and start fighting for what matters most.

According to two Web rating services, about one in four regular Internet users, or 21 million Americans, visits one of the more than sixty thousand sex sites on the Internet at least once a month—more people than go to sports or government sites.[5]

While pornography may temporarily anesthetize a man's emotional pain and provide a euphoric mood swing, he becomes like a wagon wheel that slips off an axle, rolls down a hill, and spins out of control faster and faster, until it finally hits a wall and shatters.

And we're kidding ourselves, or we're as out of touch

with reality as a carefree cow in a slaughterhouse, if we deny the extent to which followers of Jesus use this counterfeit prescription. The growth of pornography has reached epidemic proportions in the church, and no population of men is immune—including pastors, priests, counselors, elders, deacons, and lay leaders. According to an article in *New Man* magazine, one-third of all pastors struggle with Internet pornography.[6]

Spiritually passive men minimize the seriousness of such sins or deny their own vulnerability. Several years ago a leader in the church I pastored told me he could never commit a sexual sin like adultery.

"Really?" I said. "If that's true then you must be godlier than King David, wiser than Solomon, and stronger than Samson."

He stared at me for at least fifteen seconds, pushed his wire-rimmed glasses up on the bridge of his beak-like nose, and said, "I never thought of it like that."

Most men haven't. The truth is the evil one snared the godliest, wisest, and strongest men in the Old Testament with a rope perfumed with lust. He knows we're vulnerable in this area, so he instructs his troops to set up a series of temptations, like mine fields, along the path of our life.

It's no surprise that we willingly step into the noose or onto the mine. We've allowed ourselves to be pushed around by a component of the Christian culture that urges us to act less like mighty men and more like passive spectators. At the same time we're dominated by a secular culture that tells us our possessions determine our worth, and pain should be

anesthetized with sex. Brainwashed and beaten down, we allow the enemy to take what he wants the most: our heart.

I, for one, am tired of being pushed around. I'm also tired of watching other men passively fade into the background of the wallpaper hanging in Satan's office. If we're going to fulfill our God-given purpose as men, it's imperative that we stand up to these cultural bullies and start fighting for what matters most.

STAND YOUR GROUND

"So, Bill," you may say, "what matters most? What's worth fighting for?"

One of David's mighty men would have answered, "A field of beans." In fact, he risked his life fighting for that field. His name was Shammah. You'll learn more about him in the next chapter. His name meant *waste,* and for years he may have wasted his life. But one day he did something which forever set him apart as one of David's mighty men.

A Philistine army had been attacking local farmers and stealing their crops. Since the Philistines had a monopoly on iron weapons, the task proved easier than taking a bone from a toothless dog.

In the face of such overwhelming force, all the villagers fled except Shammah. Something inside this man told him God had created him to fight evil. No Philistine punks would bully him. God had given the land to Israel, and he refused to let the Philistines drive him from it. Allowing the enemy to win would be tantamount to surrendering to their idols and immoral practices. While the rest of the Jewish men

took off with their families like flying insects afraid to light anywhere for fear they'd be crushed, Shammah grabbed his sword, planted his feet in the middle of his field of beans, and said, in Clint Eastwood form, "Make my day!"

I suspect the Philistines laughed at this single warrior pathetically challenging their might. Big mistake. You see, while they may have surrounded Shammah, they had not surrounded his God. Mighty men stand their ground and fight—and they fight to win. While the rest of the community nervously peeked out from their hiding places, Shammah single-handedly routed the Philistines.

> **Mighty men stand their ground and fight—and they fight to win.**

Today our battle isn't with swords and shields. We don't take on an enemy in hand-to-hand combat in a fight to the death. Our war is against an invisible spiritual enemy and the cultural forces he uses to bully us. The apostle Paul warned us about this: "For our struggle is not against flesh and blood, but against the rulers, against the authorities, against the powers of this dark world and against the spiritual forces of evil in the heavenly realms" (Ephesians 6:12).

How do we fight such an enemy? We follow Shammah's example—we stand our ground. That's why Paul went on to say, "Therefore put on the full armor of God, so that when the day of evil comes, you may be able *to stand* your ground, and after you have done everything, *to stand*" (Ephesians 6:13, italics mine). Twice in one verse he exhorts us to stand.

I'm convinced that we discover the secret of masculine

strength when we follow God's command to stop running, stop being bullied, and stop living passive lives. We unleash the warrior within when we tap into God's power and say, "I will not be bullied any more. From this day forward I'm going to stand my ground and fight for what God values—not what the culture values. I refuse to be driven by a desire to win the marketplace war and I will no longer anesthetize my pain with illicit sex or any other harmful process or substance. I will follow the example of David's mighty men and wage war against the forces of hell that seek to destroy me and my family."

Recognizing you're engaged in a spiritual battle and deciding to stand your ground are crucial first steps. In the remaining chapters you'll discover the six battles you must win. But equally important, you'll find a biblical strategy that will assure your victory. The first and foundational battle is for your identity as a spiritual warrior. It's essential that you derive your identity from what God says about you—not what you, your experiences, or your critics say about you.

Go ahead and turn the page—you're about to enter the first battle.

Discussion Questions

1. How have some churches contributed to the feminization of men? Why do you think this has happened?

2. Do you think of the church as a place where you can be yourself? Why or why not?

3. *How has our culture taught men to find significance? How has this played out in your life?*

4. *How has our culture taught men to medicate pain? Why is this so dangerous?*

5. *What did Shammah do in the face of an enemy attack?*

6. *Are you ready to stand up to the cultural bullies and fight for what God values? Why or why not?*

BATTLE ONE

Fight for Your Identity

Some things are worth fighting for. Others are not. Often we fail to fight for the right things until they've been taken from us. I think that's one reason the movie *The Patriot* resonated with me. Set in South Carolina during the outbreak of the American Revolutionary War, a former soldier named Benjamin Martin, played by Mel Gibson, resists being drawn into the war with England. Although once a wily and ferocious soldier, he married a gracious woman who bore him seven children and urged him to trade in his violent past for a peaceful life on his sprawling plantation.

Recently widowed, Martin seeks a life of peace with his children. At one point in the movie he says, "If you're asking whether I'm willing to go to war with England, the answer is no. I've been to war, and I have no desire to do so again." In an emotional address to the Charleston Assembly

he declares, "I have seven children. My wife is dead. Who's to care for them if I go to war?"

With the conflict breaking out all around, Martin's eldest son, Gabriel, enlists with the Continental army. His unit is quickly routed after a major battle only a few miles from his father's plantation. Seeking to stay neutral, Martin offers medical care for the injured British and American soldiers who lie wounded all over his front lawn. In "appreciation" British Colonel William Tavington savagely kills Martin's second eldest son, hauls Gabriel off to be hanged, and burns down Martin's farm because he harbored the enemy.

> Some things are worth fighting for. Others are not. Often we fail to fight for the right things until they've been taken from us.

That single moment changes everything for Benjamin Martin—like the bombing of Pearl Harbor or the terrorist attack of 9/11 did for the United States. From that moment forward Martin knows that passivity will not quell his enemy nor protect his family. His only recourse is to fight. Once the warrior is awakened, Martin leads the patriots with a wild-eyed fury.

The warrior within me is aroused by Martin's loss. I feel his anger and determination. I celebrate his courage in the face of a cruel enemy. But I'm convinced the source of my feelings goes deeper than that. I value some people and relationships so much that I would fight to the death for them. Unlike Martin, I want to fight before I lose them—not after.

But what, exactly, are the values we should stand our

ground and fight for? As warriors we must know the answer to this question. I'm convinced the first battle involves our identity in Christ. All else flows from that.

WHAT'S IN A NAME?

I laughed out loud the first time I saw the cartoon. It featured a smiling golden retriever with a caption above his head that read, "Hi. My name is No! No! Bad Dog! What's yours?" The poor dog had been yelled at so many times he concluded his name was "No! No! Bad Dog!"

Imagine not only having someone call you a degrading name—that's happened to the best of us—but actually having your parents give you a degrading name. One of the mighty men of the Bible was named Josheb-Basshebeth[1] (unless your tongue's a gymnast, it's difficult to pronounce), which means *shame*. And we've already touched on the one named Shammah, which means *waste* (2 Samuel 23:8, 11).

I have no idea why their parents gave them such demeaning names. Perhaps life had ground them down to a nub and they didn't think their children could amount to much. Maybe the weight of hardship had grown so unbearable that they unloaded the boulders of grief onto the backs of their sons. A contemporary parallel might be a crack baby who enters the world crippled by his mother's addiction or the child of an alcoholic who daily suffers verbal abuse and name-calling.

As I reflected on the names of those two warriors and the implied pain of their childhood, I recalled my own. Both my parents were alcoholics. They married and divorced

each other numerous times. Their attempts to patch things together created a marriage as ugly as Frankenstein's monster. On one occasion, while they were trying to figure out what to do with their lives, they dumped me in an orphanage. I wasn't yet four years old and the memories are vague, like a forgotten nightmare.

But I do remember the emotions. I recall feeling unwanted and frightened, like a dog driven away by his master and afraid to get close to his new one. Later, when my parents reunited and I returned home, I recall the feelings of shame I associated with our family. While we lived in a large house, I didn't want my friends to visit for fear they would see my parents drunk or fighting.

At night, before falling asleep, I entered a dream world where I imagined myself as a champion. I knew the thrill of throwing a touchdown-scoring pass. I knew how it felt to graduate number one in my class. Sometimes my dreams would continue on for days or weeks. I clung to the hope that one day I would be a champion.

It's no wonder I identified with these two mighty men. As I considered their story I wondered if they too created such childhood dreams. Did they cling to fantasies of greatness that helped them endure the pain of life?

DEALING WITH OUR WOUNDS

What about you? Can you identify with those warriors? Have you suffered rejection? Have you had people you admire look down at you like an arrogant maître d' at a trendy restaurant? Have those you love minimized your gifts and

talents? Have they ridiculed your dreams or reminded you of past failures?

I remember craving my dad's attention as a boy. More than anything else my dad wanted me to excel athletically. He had visions of me playing professional football—or at least competing at the collegiate level. Apart from the fact that I was too small, too slow, too weak, and had a low tolerance for pain, I probably would have made it.

> In God's economy scars are the preparation for greatness.

Of course, when kids are young, most can compete if they give it their best shot. And because I worked hard and out-hustled every other kid, I seemed destined for greatness. That changed the night I ran back a kickoff during a "big" ninth-grade game and blew out my right knee. Back in those days orthopedic surgeons fixed torn ligaments and cartilage by gutting the knee and sewing it up.

My dad never seemed to grasp the fact that without an ACL (anterior cruciate ligament) in my right knee, I had no lateral movement. Basically, whenever I would cut to the left my knee would buckle and I'd fall to the ground, writhing in pain. What I lacked in size, speed, and knee strength, I made up for with a survival instinct that told me, "If you stop playing football you'll stop hurting."

When I retired from the gridiron at age sixteen my dad offered me this bit of insight aimed at encouraging me to give it one more try: "The problem isn't your knee," he said. "The problem is you're a quitter."

At that point I knew that I would probably never win my dad's blessing. The pain of that reality hurt far worse than my knee, and it still does.

I'm sure you too have been deeply wounded. Maybe you've allowed the scars from such wounds to paralyze your potential and render you as motionless as a toy soldier. I'd like to suggest that in God's economy these painful experiences are preparation for greatness. Such wounds are the material God uses to build mighty men of faith. You must let him, not your past failures or present scars, define you.

The Bible is filled with stories of men who suffered before God used them.

Moses was called a murderer and spent forty years in the wilderness before delivering the Israelites from Pharaoh. Yet he's remembered today as a deliverer, and a great man of faith.

Joseph was sold as a slave by his brothers and later spent time in an Egyptian prison after being accused of attempted sexual assault. All of this before Pharaoh elevated him to a position of leadership. What comes to your mind when you hear the name *Joseph*? Do you regard him as an accused rapist or a brilliant and godly leader? The struggles Joseph faced strengthened his character and prepared him for his role as a great leader.

Peter acted as a coward by denying Christ before becoming a pillar of the church. Today we acknowledge his shortcomings but view him as a powerful man of faith.

So what's in a name? Everything! But names can be changed or added to. David took a man named "Shame" and

one named "Waste" and called them mighty men. Regardless of your name—given by your parents or your tormenters—in the eyes of God, you're a mighty man of faith. That's your true identity according to the God who created you and dwells within you. If that wasn't so, why would the apostle Paul command you to put on God's armor and stand against the devil (Ephesians 6:13)?

Living like a warrior demands that you embrace the inevitability of hardship rather than fleeing from it. Pause a moment and contemplate this truth. Hardship often brings you to your lowest point, and in the process, tempts you to see yourself as less than a mighty man of God. Your tendency will be to attempt to avoid suffering altogether or see it as an aberration. Neither approach will help because neither is grounded in reality.

WHEN THIN ICE BREAKS

Life is tough. There's nothing we can do to completely protect us from suffering—not prayer, not fasting, not Bible reading, nothing. Like lightning, hardship will strike and we won't know when or where until after it hits us.

We like to think times of health, wealth, and tension-free relationships are the norm. In such a world cars never break down. The worst health problem we face is an occasional headache. And the biggest fight is over who forgot to take out the trash. Like children who believe in fairy tales, we cling to the illusion that prosperity, peace, and good health are the norm.

This type of thinking reminds me of a time when I

played a round of golf with a friend. I couldn't help but be impressed with the power and grace of his swing. The only thing more impressive was the distance he drove the ball.

With each hit the ball compressed and then took off as though shot from a howitzer. What bothered him, however, was the fact that he couldn't correct a nasty slice. Every time the ball lazily arched away from the fairway and into a stand of firs or a field of tall grass, he would slam his driver on the ground and growl.

> Living like a warrior means embracing the inevitability of hardship rather than fleeing from it.

After one especially bothersome slice, I offered him a golfing tip: "Rod, I think you'd enjoy the game more if you embraced the fact that bad drives are as much a part of your game as good ones. The way I see it, you believe that those loooong straight drives are the norm. And . . ."

"And you don't think they are?" he said.

"Yeah, that's right," I said. "It just seems to me the bad shots are as much a part of your game as the good ones. I know I'm a hacker. I accept that. So when I occasionally happen to hit the ball in the fairway, it's both a surprise and a celebration."

Rod shook his head and growled something under his breath as he climbed into the cart. The moment I sat beside him we both erupted into laughter. Of course, Rod does realize bad shots are a part of his golf game. Unfortunately, most of us haven't accepted the fact that bad days, bad decisions, and broken relationships are as much

a part of life as bad weather. When we encounter them we're tempted to think God doesn't care, so we write him off. And in that moment the enemy has planted his flag in our heart.

I'm convinced we would do better with life if we realized that life is tough. It's hard. There are seasons of life that seem unbearable. All too often we see champions of the faith and think they have avoided such hardship. But they haven't. They've embraced it, as every athlete embraces the pain of rigorous training. They refuse to allow setbacks to shape their identity.

STRENGTHENED BY HARDSHIP

All of David's mighty men were veterans in the war with disappointment and pain. The biblical text tells us they were "in distress," "in debt," or "discontented" when they joined David (1 Samuel 22:2).

Their lives had fallen through thin ice and dropped into a cold darkness. They had lost their money, their homes, and their reputations. Like undersized children, they had been pushed around by a school-yard bully named Saul who tirelessly sought to dishonor and destroy them as they fled with David from Saul's wrath.

The more I reflected on these men, the more their story captured my imagination. My own loss of a vision, in which I had invested eleven years, ate away at me like a tapeworm, consuming my strength and with it my hope. Yet I sensed there was something about these men that would help me, if only I could see it. Over and over again I told myself:

These men who suffered so much were David's mighty men! An insight—something important—kept eluding my grasp.

And then I had a realization that caused everything to fall into place—like a math problem that suddenly makes sense. The identity of a warrior isn't destroyed by adversity, it's strengthened.

The identity of a warrior isn't destroyed by adversity, it's strengthened.

As I reflect on that insight now it almost seems trite. But in that moment, because of my sorrow, it was a lifeline thrown to a drowning man. I realized that this elemental truth had evaded me because I was too proud, or simply unwilling, to embrace it. In that moment, failure had stripped away my pride and God had brought me to a place where I could grab hold of it.

I realized that the God-given masculinity of these mighty men didn't wither under the hot sun of hardship. It emerged. They found God's stability at their time of greatest need, like a tree with deep roots during a gale. In him they discovered a source of strength that let them stand tall.

That means all the hardship we've suffered can be used by God to make us stronger, not weaker. It means if you've suffered or are suffering, God wants to use adversity to mold you into a mighty man of faith.

Perhaps you accept the validity of such an idea but aren't sure how it works. It seems that when a loss exposes our weakness and we run to God, we discover his strength. You see, God's power is unleashed at the point of your

greatest weakness. That's why Paul declared, "When I am weak, then I am strong" (2 Corinthians 12:10).

The benefits of this reality are profound. If during times of weakness you turn to God, you'll emerge a stronger man because you'll rely on his strength, not your own. Your identity will be dependent on him, not on your circumstances. In doing so you'll stand shoulder to shoulder with other men whom God empowered to fight against spiritual darkness. Consider these biblical heroes:

Elijah was hunted by an evil king and queen . . . but he sparked a revival.

Daniel was thrown into a lions' den . . . and God delivered him.

Paul was persecuted . . . but wrote much of the New Testament.

The list of biblical warriors who became strong through adversity goes on and on and on. God used suffering to expose their weaknesses and drive them to him so that in his power they could attack enemy strongholds. Ultimately, God wants to use our vulnerabilities to help us find our identity in his strength. The choice is ours. When we're broken and our weakness is exposed we can see ourselves as powerless and unable to fight. Or we can acknowledge our weakness. Instead of letting it define our identity, we can allow God's strength—manifested in our weakness—to define us.

Maybe the hardship you're currently experiencing has made you feel as hopeless as a sky diver with a shredded parachute. Or it could be you've gotten used to calling yourself "average" or "nothing special."

A little over a decade ago I was invited by Bill Hybels, senior pastor at Willow Creek Community Church, to join a small group of emerging church leaders for a strategy retreat in Arizona. I felt honored and hoped God would continue to prosper my pastoring efforts with numerical growth as he had done in the past. Instead, he allowed me to serve in a ministry that remained small in numbers for over a decade. I knew that I had disappeared from the radar screen of those looking for point men in rapidly expanding ministries. I no longer possessed the credentials that identified me as a "make-it-happen guy." I had somehow withered in the eyes of others and in my own eyes too.

> God does not, nor did he ever, see you as insignificant. Nor has he overlooked you.

Only a few years earlier I had been offered the pastorate of one of the leading churches in the San Francisco Bay area. I had been urged to conduct church-growth seminars. At the end of that disappointing decade I felt fully qualified to conduct seminars for pastors who had poured out their hearts, loved their congregations, preached tirelessly, and implemented creative church-growth strategies only to see their church sit as motionless as a clipper ship on a windless day. I knew the pain of having others blame the lack of growth on poor leadership, unconfessed sin, or an absence of prayer. And I know how it hurts to feel small and insignificant, because I allowed the words of critics and the agony of disappointment to define me.

Have you known such feelings? Do they haunt you now? If so, it's crucial for you to remember that God does not, nor did he ever, see you as insignificant. Nor has he overlooked you. On the contrary, he views you as one of the most powerful warriors on this planet. To think otherwise is to believe a lie. And it's essential for you to realize that suffering and disappointment are God's way of exposing your weakness so you can find your identity in his strength.

Remember the men named "Waste" and "Shame" who became two of David's key supporters? Regardless of how bleak your past or present may look, as a man, you're a warrior engaged against the forces of hell in a war of eternal value. That's your true identity. You're fighting for your heart and the hearts of your family. God wired you to do battle and offers you his unlimited strength to assure your victory. Once you embrace that truth, you'll be ready to draw nearer to God and fight the second battle.

Discussion Questions

1. *What are the deepest and most painful wounds you've suffered?*

2. *How do disappointment and pain adversely affect a man's identity?*

3. *In what way can God use your weakness to strengthen your identity in him? (You may want to read 2 Corinthians 12:7-10 for additional insight.)*

4. Why is God's strength found in your weakness? How will this prepare you for future spiritual battles?

5. In spite of the disappointments you've faced, how does God view you?

CHAPTER FIVE

BATTLE TWO

Fight for Personal Holiness

For centuries the garments of European rulers and judges have been lined with ermine fur. The story behind that custom highlights one of the most unusual behaviors in the animal kingdom.

An ermine is a cute little animal with shiny black eyes and beautiful fur. It has short legs and a narrow body that's some twenty inches long from the tip of its nose to the end of its tail. The agile animal is found in the northern region of the northern hemisphere. In summer, its coat is a rich chocolate brown except for the undersides of the body and legs. In winter, the color changes to a clear white, broken only by a black tip on the tail.

If you looked up a picture of the ermine at the library, you would be shocked by the purity of its white fur. The ermine seems to realize the beauty of its coat and takes great pride

in maintaining it. Indeed, the animal's most unusual characteristic is its hatred of anything that might soil its fur.

Hunters who know this will fill an ermine's burrow with filth and wait with their dogs for the furry animal to return. Once the ermine spots the dogs, the snow-white creature will dart for the safety of its burrow. But the ermine will not enter the soiled safety of its home. Rather than flee into the burrow, the ermine will fight the dogs to the death. It would rather die with a bloodstained coat than live with a dirty one.

We need to realize personal holiness is a value worth fighting for.

That's why the ermine's fur is used on the robes of rulers and judges. It serves as a symbol of the purity of justice and law.

Don't you find it amazing that God programmed an ermine to prefer a fight to the death over a soiled coat? Its instinct for purity outweighs its survival instinct.

Mighty men need a similar instinct. We need to realize personal holiness is a value worth fighting for—in fact, it's the second battle every man must win. I'm convinced it's also a battle we won't enter into until we understand the holiness of our God and the holiness he has given us through his Son.

A CLOSE ENCOUNTER WITH GOD

I find it fascinating that so many science fiction movies depict alien starships landing on the earth in a magnificent display of light. In the classic 1977 Steven Spielberg film *Close Encounters of the Third Kind,* the climactic scene

takes place at the foot of the Devil's Tower National Monument at Devil's Tower, Wyoming.

As a crowd of scientists and other spectators gaze into the sky, an immense alien mother ship appears—a circular mass twice the size of Devil's Tower, with thousands of glittering, illuminated windows. The people in the crowd stand with mouths agape as the enormous vessel dwarfs the Tower, revolves, and slowly descends toward them. It is staggeringly beautiful as it lands. The light from the ship is so bright that the onlookers must wear dark glasses. The great space vessel finally touches down at the end of the runway, and when a door opens, it reveals an interior flooded with light. The crowd can't see what is inside, but they know it's a higher being.

This image was so compelling that as I watched the film, I wanted to run up the ramp and into the ship. Like other people, I crave an encounter with a being superior to and different from me. A person so wonderful the only visual image that could capture his essence is light.

There is such a Being: God is the reality men seek in the extraterrestrial. He exists apart from and above his creation. Perhaps that's why the word "holy" is used more often as a prefix to God's name than any other attribute.

Most people believe the words *holy* and *pure* are synonymous. They aren't. The word *holy* describes the essence of all of God's moral attributes, of which purity is an element. When Isaiah beheld God sitting on his throne, high and exalted, with his robe filling the temple, angels flew around him and said to one another, "Holy, holy, holy is the

Lord Almighty; the whole earth is full of his glory" (Isaiah 6:3). The angels didn't say the Lord is powerful, pure, loving, just, or merciful. They said he is holy. The word describes the sum of all of God's moral excellence.

If I were asked to describe the sun I would say, "The sun is bright." Why? Because *brightness* describes the essence of all of the sun's characteristics: hot, burning, gaseous, and explosive. Brightness is to the sun what holiness is to God.

While the word *holy* describes the essence of all of God's attributes, the primary meaning of holy is "separate." Not separate in the sense of being "apart from" but in the sense of possessing a "superior excellence." We might say that an excellent diamond, sports car, or team is set apart. It's in a class of its own.

But God's holiness is more than just separate; it's also transcendent.[1] Webster tells us the word *transcendent* means "going beyond ordinary limits, surpassing, exceeding."[2] God is above and beyond all of his creation. The more we focus on God, the more everything else fades away, like the frame around a picture.

So how does the holiness of God relate to evil? Remember, we're engaged in a war between good and evil, between a holy God and an unholy army of demons, between servants of God and enemies of God. Nobody is neutral in this conflict. Nobody.

Because God is intrinsically holy, evil can no more invade his being than darkness can infiltrate light. Who ever heard of a black beam of darkness shooting across a brightly lit room? Because God is light he lives unpolluted by evil. He

possesses eternal innocence in his nature and in his deeds. No wonder the apostle John wrote, "God is light; in him there is no darkness at all" (1 John 1:5). He sees evil all around him in his fallen creation but dispels it as light does darkness.

God is not only separate from evil, he hates sin in all of its manifestations. I've often wondered what that must be like. There are foods I hate and refuse to taste, like liver. I don't care if it's fried with onions or marinated in the most delicious French sauce, I hate liver and refuse to take a single bite of it. But that illustration breaks down because it's not just that God hates the taste of sin—it's the extreme opposite of his nature. God is light, and evil is darkness. Or to put it differently, he repels evil like the positive ends of two magnets repel each other.

God repels evil like the positive ends of two magnets repel each other.

THE BATTLE FOR HOLINESS

One night while running from King Saul and three thousand of his troops, David faced a heart-wrenching decision. Under the cover of darkness, David and Abishai, one of his mighty men, stealthily entered the king's camp. Surrounded by his sleeping men, the king slept as soundly as a baby.

Abishai saw the moment as a divine appointment. "Today God has delivered your enemy into your hands," he said (1 Samuel 26:8). He pleaded with David to let him kill the king with a single thrust of his spear. "I won't strike him twice," he said.

Overhead the stars blinked. In the distance a wolf howled. Closer, much closer, angels leaned forward and watched as David contemplated Abishai's request. I wonder what ran through David's mind in that moment between hearing and answering. Perhaps he thought, *With Saul dead, I could take his crown. My days of fear, despair, running, and hiding would be ended. I could right the wrongs this ruthless man has perpetrated against me.*

> David served a holy God, and doing so meant he had to separate himself from all evil.

Whether or not David entertained such thoughts we'll never know. What we do know is that the leader of the mighty men told Abishai, "Don't destroy him! Who can lay a hand on the Lord's anointed and be guiltless?" (I Samuel 26:9).

Like a compass on a dark night, God's holiness directed the fugitive. David served a holy God, and doing so meant he had to separate himself from all evil . . . even evil that might momentarily feel good and make life easier.

And what of his mighty man, Abishai? How did he respond to David's reference to God's anointed? Without a moment's hesitation, he stepped back.

I hope this profound act of courage doesn't slip by you unnoticed. In that moment Abishai proved he was a mighty man. Not because he killed the king or his army, but because he bridled his own lust for revenge. Saul had chased David and his men for years, forcing them into a nomadic life away from Israelite society, yet Abishai acted as a warrior who serves a holy God. He refused to sin when

sinning seemed so justified. In that moment he fought like a man who realized the real war wasn't against Saul, but against the evil forces that sought to capture his heart and compromise his holiness.

David and Abishai had the courage to obey God even when it exposed them to greater danger. They would rather do right and stand with God than do wrong and stand against him. Such actions flow from the supernatural courage that a holy God gives his holy warriors.

No man can look at the face of God without beholding his holiness any more than he can look at the sun without seeing its brightness. And upon seeing God's holiness, men become acutely aware of their humanity. The holiness that David sensed on that dark night, Isaiah beheld years later in a vision. When the prophet saw God's holiness he cried out, "Woe to me! . . . I am ruined! For I am a man of unclean lips, and I live among a people of unclean lips, and my eyes have seen the King, the Lord Almighty" (Isaiah 6:5).

Like Isaiah, the more clearly I see the holiness of God, the more clearly I see my own sinfulness. In Isaiah's case, an angel flew to him with a hot coal that he had taken with tongs from the altar. He touched the prophet's mouth and said, "See, this has touched your lips; your guilt is taken away and your sin atoned for" (Isaiah 6:7).

TRANSFORMED BY GOD'S HOLINESS

Apart from God nothing is holy in itself. For objects or people to be holy, God must sanctify them (set them apart). He must make them holy. Just as the legendary King Midas

had the power to touch something and turn it into gold, so God's touch transforms men from the commonplace into something special, different, and set apart.

That's exactly what he's done to every Christian. Through faith in Jesus, we've been identified with him in his death, burial, and resurrection. (I'll discuss this more in chapter nine.) Because of this, the apostle Paul said we are the temple of the Holy Spirit (1 Corinthians 6:19). That means God's Spirit now lives within us. Peter said, "But you are a chosen people, a royal priesthood, a holy nation, a people belonging to God" (1 Peter 2:9). There is a sense in which we will never be holier than we are the moment we first trust Christ. Theologians call this "positional holiness." Our responsibility is to allow what is on the inside to work its way out in our lives—this is referred to as "progressive holiness."

When a fax machine receives a message, once the transfer of information is complete, the fax machine possesses all the data it will ever receive from that transmission. But only after the transmission is complete does the invisible message get transferred onto paper so it can be seen. That process illustrates the relationship between positional and progressive holiness. The moment we trust Christ as our Savior, God makes us righteous—holy—in his sight. We spend the remainder of our lives allowing the holiness we possess in him to be transferred onto the paper of our thoughts, words, and deeds.

Our goal should be a perfect correspondence between God's *unseen* holiness within us and *evident* holiness in

our lifestyle. We progressively become living expressions of the holy God who lives within us. The degree to which we understand our new identity is the degree to which we will think and act like Jesus and others will see him in our lives. Our thoughts, words, and deeds reveal the depth of our comprehension of all we are and have in Christ.

As holy men, we must allow our minds and bodies to be used in a pure way. Nobody would put on a five-hundred-dollar suit before mowing the grass or working in the garden. Similarly, we have been made holy by God. As holy men we should live consistently with our new nature.

> God's touch transforms men from the commonplace into something special, different, and set apart.

Peter emphasized this when he said, "As obedient children, do not conform to the evil desires you had when you lived in ignorance. But just as he who called you is holy, so be holy in all you do; for it is written: 'Be holy, because I am holy' " (1 Peter 1:14-16).

True masculinity isn't found in gratifying our base desires for money, power, and sex. That's nothing more than denying our new identity and allowing our flesh to rule our heart. True masculinity is found in the person of Jesus Christ and our identity in him. Every day of our life we must grow in the knowledge of our holy God. And every day we must fight against our fleshly appetites that drive us to conform to our culture rather than to the holiness of the God who indwells us.

It's only as we stand our ground on this truth and fight for personal holiness that we will be prepared to win the

next battle—the battle for our family. You see, the more God's holiness captures our heart at a conscious level, the more eagerly we'll fight for the hearts of our family. If you're single, pray God will equip you now to wage such warfare in the future if you should marry. In a sense, how diligently we fight for our family reveals the depth of our knowledge of God's holiness and the holiness he's imparted to us.

Because God wants your wife and children to have hearts filled with his holiness, it's crucial that you read the next chapter and learn how to fight for your family like a mighty man of God.

Discussion Questions

1. What does the word holy mean? How is God holy?

2. Because God is holy, how does he relate to evil?

3. How did David's view of God affect his decision not to kill Saul? (2 Samuel 26:8-9)

4. How have followers of Christ received the holiness of God (1 Corinthians 6:19; 1 Peter 2:9)? How should this affect the battle for your heart (1 Peter 1:14-16)?

5. List some ways you can stand your ground and fight for personal holiness.

CHAPTER SIX

BATTLE THREE

Fight for Your Family

I find it distressing but not surprising that according to the Barna Research Group, professing Christians are just as likely to get divorced as unbelievers.[1] I realize there are a host of reasons for the breakdown of marriages among Christians. But I'm convinced, after counseling hundreds of couples for more than two decades, that a major factor in the failure of marriages is the passivity of men.

That reality is both good news and bad news. The good news is that a husband's decision to provide his wife with spiritual leadership and emotional nurturing can infuse a marriage with vitality. The bad news is that passive men don't usually act until a marital explosion gets their attention—and then it's often too late.

My wife, Cindy, and I had only been married for a couple of years when our relationship shattered. She would say I

had become an insensitive and uncaring jerk—an assessment that seemed extreme to me. I felt she was a bit too sensitive.

At the time, I was attending seminary, leading a Young Life club, and helping start a new church. I didn't have a lot of time left over for Cindy.

While driving home from my classes one day I had the following conversation with God:

"Please fix Cindy."

No answer.

"Please show me how I can fix Cindy."

No answer.

Desperate, I pleaded with God. "I'll do anything. Just tell me what you want me to do."

In that moment a passage from the Bible seared itself onto my heart. I had read the passage countless times. I had memorized it. I had studied it in the original language. I had attended a seminar in which someone else had dissected the verse and explained its meaning. But while I was driving my car on the Dallas/Fort Worth freeway, God used that verse, like a farmer's plow, to soften my hard heart.

The sixteen words were simply: "Husbands, love your wives, just as Christ loved the church and gave himself up for her" (Ephesians 5:25).

God wanted me to love Cindy sacrificially. That meant I had to put effort into our relationship, not sit back and assume it would take care of itself. Looking back, I realize God performed a supernatural work that day. At the core of my being I determined to obey God. Before arriving home

I identified three major changes I needed to make in the way I treated my wife:

1. Take time every day to listen to her with my full attention.
2. Pray with her every day.
3. Show her nonsexual affection every day.

I told God that, by his grace, I would practice these changes every day for one month. (I figured I could keep that commitment.) I also told him that if it didn't make a radical difference in our marriage we would see a counselor. Of course, I told Cindy none of this since I figured that at that time she would trust me about as much as she would trust a politician's promise.

A month later, when I told her about my conversation with God, I didn't need to convince her that I had meant business. She already knew. And I had learned a valuable lesson: my active love and leadership are the keys to a happy wife and a fulfilling marriage. Of course, after years of marriage I've discovered I periodically struggle with passivity and have to recommit myself to actively loving my wife. Fortunately, since I know the warning signs, the periods of passivity don't last as long and the damage isn't as severe.

Perhaps my insight seems a bit simplistic. But I guarantee

> I guarantee you, your marriage will thrive if you consciously choose to love your wife as Christ loved the church and daily put her needs before your own.

you, your marriage will thrive if you consciously choose to love your wife as Christ loved the church and daily put her needs before your own. That doesn't mean if it's sick today it will automatically be healthy tomorrow, next week, or next month. But in time it will prosper.* And if you're single this truth will prepare you for marriage.

FIGHT FOR YOUR WIFE

The critical issue for most men rests on a decision to value their wife and love her sacrificially one day at a time. That daily decision is as crucial to the health of your marriage as was Shammah's decision to defend his field of beans.

If any of David's mighty men questioned their leader's commitment to his family and theirs, they found the answer wrapped in smoke and written in soot. While returning to Ziklag, a village they had made their home, the exhausted men longed for their families. But while they were still miles away, they saw smoke billowing into the sky.

Once in Ziklag they found a terrible scene—a village so desolate, so battered, so burned it assaulted credulity. Where there should have been smiling wives and laughing children, the terrain belched smoke. The overwhelming magnitude of their loss threw the men to the ground, where they wept until they were too exhausted to weep.

Grief soon erupted into anger and the men considered stoning their leader. David turned to God, who told him to pursue the raiders and promised him success. Driven by a

---

*Sometimes a husband can love his wife sacrificially by agreeing to see a therapist, read a marriage book, or attend a seminar.

love for their families and a confidence in God, the men pursued their enemies and engaged them in a ferocious battle that lasted a night and a day. Finally, every raider lay dead except those who had fled on camels.

As the sun snuggled up to the western horizon, David and his men searched for their families. The biblical text tells us, "Nothing was missing: young or old, boy or girl, plunder or anything else they had taken. David brought everything back" (1 Samuel 30:19).

Hundreds of men were reunited with their wives and children. Every man who embraced his wife did so because he was willing to sacrifice his life for her.

I believe I would have fought beside those men—wouldn't you? Most men would die for their wife. The bigger challenge is living for her. Such sacrificial love isn't easy to practice because it requires choosing to put her before yourself one day at a time. That's no doubt why the apostle Peter told husbands to live with their wives in "an understanding way" and treat them with "honor" (1 Peter 3:7, NASB). God wants you to have insight into the way your wife thinks and feels so you can be aware of her needs and meet them.

If you wonder how you're doing, ask your wife these questions:

- Do you feel I give you my undivided attention when you're talking to me?
- Do I show you enough nonsexual affection?
- Do you think we pray together enough?
- Do we spend enough time together?

Curious as to my own performance, I recently asked Cindy these questions. She smiled and said, "You haven't arrived yet."

These aren't sophisticated questions that need deciphering by a code breaker. If your wife indicates you need to work on these areas, you'll find they aren't complex activities that require years of coaching. What they do demand is a determination to allow Jesus to live through you and enable you to love your wife sacrificially. And they require that you throw away passivity like a dull razor.

> **Most men would die for their wife. The bigger challenge is living for her.**

Such sacrificial love serves a high purpose. Jesus gave himself for the church so that he might "make her holy, cleansing her by the washing with water through the word, and to present her to himself as a radiant church, without stain or wrinkle or any other blemish" (Ephesians 5:26-27).

Our aim should be to love our wife in order to strengthen her spiritually. We must fight for her heart as we do our own. Our passion should be to have a cleansing effect on her so that both her thoughts and actions are pure. We must serve as her "spiritual windshield wiper"—continually removing anything that blurs her vision and threatens her safety.

I grieve the fact that I too often forget the high value God places on my wife and the honor he wants me to give her. At times I treat her like a used Pinto rather than a shiny new Porsche. I find a reminder of her value in Genesis 2:22.

It's there we read that God "built" Eve from a rib he took from Adam's side.

The Hebrew word for "built" is the same one used in reference to God building his sanctuary (Psalm 78:69) and a house (Psalm 127:1). It's also the word used when speaking of the construction of Solomon's palace (1 Kings 7:1-2).

Before you move past this too quickly, consider the fact that each of these building projects flowed from a plan aimed at meeting a specific need. The same is true of Eve. God designed her so that she would meet Adam's need for companionship—and so he would also meet her need. Nothing in all of creation compared with the work of genius God demonstrated when he created Adam. And I believe he exceeded that masterpiece when he built Eve and brought her to Adam. In my estimation, nothing in all of creation matches the beauty of a woman.

No wonder Solomon said, "He who finds a wife finds what is good and receives favor from the Lord" (Proverbs 18:22). He must have realized this truth in a fresh way when he looked upon his bride and said, "How beautiful you are, my darling! Oh, how beautiful!" (Song of Songs 1:15).

In his book *The Man Who Mistook His Wife for a Hat*, Dr. Oliver Sacks, a neurologist, tells the story about a man who suffered from a disorder called *visual agnosia*. Dr. P., an accomplished musician and teacher, possessed excellent musical and reasoning skills. But because he had visual agnosia he often mistook one object, or body part, for something or someone else.

Dr. Sacks recounted the first time the two met at his

clinic. During the examination Dr. Sacks had his patient remove a shoe so he could perform a reflex test on the sole of his foot. Once the test was completed, Dr. P. could not put his shoe back on because he thought his shoe was his foot and his foot his shoe.

A more surprising mistake occurred later when Dr. P. thought the examination was over and he started to look around for his hat. He "reached out his hand and took hold of his wife's head, tried to lift it off, to put it on. He had apparently mistaken his wife for a hat!" And how did his wife respond? Oliver Sacks related, "His wife looked as if she was used to such things."[2]

I'm not sure which is sadder: a man who thinks his wife is a hat, or a wife accustomed to such treatment. Sometimes I think we men fail to see our wives as masterpieces of God's creation. While we may not treat them like hats, we don't treat them like fellow heirs of the gracious gift of life (I Peter 3:7). And tragically, they often become used to such treatment.

While Dr. Sacks found no cure for Dr. P.'s malady, that need not be the case for our marriages. We can determine to stand our ground and fight the spiritual battles necessary to love our wife as Christ loved the church. We must diligently choose to put her needs before our own. We must daily see her as a fellow heir of God's grace. It's crucial for us to remember that we're each fighting a battle, not only for our own heart, but for those of our wife and children as well. And you are the only man with the God-given responsibility to protect the heart of your wife.

FIGHT FOR YOUR CHILDREN

It's impossible to adequately communicate the need your children have for your blessing. Nobody provides us with a better role model than Jesus.

Mobbed by spectators and guarded by his disciples, Jesus took the time to welcome and bless a group of children. The Greek word for "bless" means "to speak well of" or "to praise someone."[3] In Old Testament times a blessing transferred a good thing from one person to another. When Isaac, under God's direction, blessed Jacob, he imparted the promise of bountiful crops, many servants, and leadership in the family (Genesis 27:27-29).

While we may not have the ability to give a blessing of such benefits, our blessings and words of affirmation can pass on valuable gifts to our children.[4] The sense of security and destiny they receive from you will fortify their hearts when they face the enemy.

There are three ways we can bless our children:

- *Verbal affirmation:* Words of affection and approval. We should speak many more words of approval and support than words of correction or criticism.
- *Physical affirmation:* A hand on the shoulder, a pat on the back, or a hug. Wrestling with them.
- *Predictive affirmation:* Words that foresee a bright future that's consistent with their personal strengths. Each evening as I tucked my young sons into bed I'd try to take a few minutes to talk with them about their future. I assured my oldest, "God is going to use your love for

different cultures to reach many people." To my second I said, "Your creativity and ability to make friends will enable you to touch many people for God's kingdom." To my youngest I said, "Your discipline and leadership ability will open many doors of influence for you."

Such acts of affirmation are crucial because they tell our children we love them and believe God has something special for them.

As a boy I used to wear my dad's shoes and pretend I could fill them. I studied his walk and mimicked it. I adored my dad and wanted, more than anything, to be like him.

That's why I loved sports and fighting. My dad used to box professionally, and nothing pleased him more than for me to meet a kid after school in an alley. That's also why I became the class clown and spent more time in the principal's office than any other student in school—my dad laughed at my misbehavior.

> Our blessings and words of affirmation can pass on valuable gifts to our children.

After I moved out of my parents' home to attend college, I pretty much disconnected from my dad. Or he disconnected from me; I'm not sure which best describes what happened. I finished college, graduated from seminary, pastored a church in Houston, and then, twenty years ago, moved to Oregon. For the first thirteen years I lived in Oregon, I called my dad every week or two.

Seven years ago my dad, due to failing health, moved

in with my family. I celebrated, certain we would connect on a deeper level. It never happened. Instead, after a few months he called me into his room and said, "I thought you should know, you're not my son." His words hit me in the gut like a sucker punch. Dad told me this on a weekly basis for two years, and every time it hurt. Finally he agreed to a DNA test, which proved, much to his surprise, that I was indeed his son.

As a father you play a crucial role in the battle for the heart of your children. Your affirmation and love will do more to fortify them against the enemy than you can imagine.

More than anything else I wanted my dad's affirmation. Yet every time he blessed me, he stole it away with a degrading and hurtful comment. On December 29, 2001, I drove Dad to the hospital and remained with him through the day. Sensing he would soon die, time and again he said, "Son, I love you." I appreciated his words but feared he would steal them back the next day. When they admitted Dad to a room at 4 P.M., I left him. That night a nurse from the hospital called. "Your dad's dying," she said.

On December 30 at 5:10 A.M., Dad passed away. My middle son, David, and I stood at his side with our hands on his chest when, after eighty-seven years of life, he took his last breath.

I thought it ironic that Dad blessed me and then died before he could take the blessing away. God must have been smiling.

I was uncertain how I would feel about Dad after his

death. He had wounded me deeply and often. Three days after he died I found a pair of his shoes while cleaning out his closet. I remembered wearing them as a boy. I remembered walking in his steps. And then a miracle happened—God washed away my feelings of ill will and replaced them with a childlike affection. Tears streamed down my cheeks.

I'm thankful for my dad. I appreciate the fact that he gave me a sense of humor and a sense of destiny. I still remember his rough beard and the smell of Old Spice. But I know that I do not want to wait until the last day of my life to give my sons the blessing they so desperately need from their dad.

One day you too will die. And your sons and daughters will clean out your closet. I pray that when they see your shoes and remember walking in them, they'll recall the many times you hugged them, wrestled with them, kissed them, and told them how much you love them.

As a father you play a crucial role in the battle for the hearts of your children. Your affirmation and love will do more to fortify them against the enemy than you can imagine. There is nothing your children need from you more than your blessing.

PREPARE FOR THE BATTLE

As you stand your ground and fight for:

> your identity,
> personal holiness,
> and your family,

you'll face disappointment and exhaustion. The natural tendency at such times is to retreat . . . to back down . . . to anesthetize your pain with sinful behavior. If you do so, valuable ground in your heart and the hearts of your family will be surrendered to the enemy. That's why the next chapter is so important. In it you'll learn how to win the fourth battle—how to successfully fight through pain.

Discussion Questions

1. Why do you think Christian marriages are as likely to end in divorce as non-Christian marriages?

2. How does the story of David and his mighty men fighting for their families affect you? What would you have done if you had been with David that day? Why?

3. Why should you fight for the heart of your wife (Ephesians 5:26; 1 Peter 3:7)? Why is this sometimes hard to do?

4. Why is it important, in the battle for the heart of your children, that you bless them? Did your dad bless you? What effect has this had on you?

5. How can you bless your children? Be specific.

6. How do you remember your dad? How do you want to be remembered?

BATTLE FOUR
Fight through Pain

The clock had just struck midnight when I walked outside to turn on my sprinkler system. A summer heat wave had set all sorts of records and the city had decreed that we could only water our yards between midnight and six in the morning.

Five minutes later I climbed back in bed with Cindy. "What took so long?" she asked.

I contemplated how I should answer her question. I decided on the straightforward approach. "It was the naked girl next door," I said.

That got her attention. She sat up, turned on the lamp beside the bed, and said, "What naked girl?"

"The one I just saw though our neighbor's window."

"What are you talking about?"

"As I walked across the yard I noticed our neighbors'

lights were on. Curious as to why they were up so late, I approached the fence and looked through the slats. I expected to see a handful of people playing cards. Instead I saw a young woman talking on the phone. That wouldn't have been any big deal if she had been dressed. She wasn't."

"And?"

"Well, I got a powerful adrenaline rush that glued me to the fence."

"Oh, really?"

"Only for a few seconds," I assured her. "I successfully pried myself away and here I am."

Much to my surprise, Cindy didn't seem too concerned. Later, when I asked her why she responded that way, she said, "You told me the truth. Besides that, I could see you were troubled and I knew you'd take care of it."

The following morning I shared my experience with the men's small group I met with every Saturday. What happened next gave me a bigger shock than the one I had experienced the night before: Two of the four men confessed that they also had female neighbors they could see through a window at night. Both men had been watching their neighbor for years.

I felt like kicking myself. How could I have been so blind? Since I hadn't struggled with such strong cravings for years I assumed that my four friends also had their appetites under control. Two of them didn't.

These were mature men with loving families. They were guys others looked to as role models. But they both had a problem as dangerous as a tumor.

WHAT'S BEHIND THE MASK?

I shared that story in one of my previous books, *When Good Men Are Tempted,* but I tell it again here because it's so crucial. My friends' revelation made me realize the church has a serious issue that few people talk about. Within each public person we see is another private person we can't see. The outer shell isn't the true person—only a covering behind which the true person lives. We dangerously assume the two correspond, but they often don't.

There are men, even church leaders, hooked on all sorts of sinful behaviors and they don't know how to get free. What's more, they're afraid to mention their struggle for fear of rejection. Consequently, their inner person lives behind a façade of spirituality that hides their true identity. Appearing whole and free, they live in the grip of a secret life that gives them all the power of a skeleton in a knight's armor.

Fortunately, my two friends found freedom from voyeurism, although it took one of them several years. They're free but still vulnerable. Even today, many years later, they're susceptible in that area.

Within each public person is another private person we can't see.

One thing's for sure: there are a lot of men like my friends. Maybe you're one of them. Like the space shuttle *Columbia,* you appear flawless on the outside. But the impact of secret acts has weakened the hull of your spiritual integrity. You fear that when your life comes under pressure, you'll break apart, and nobody will be able to help.

If we're going to be mighty men who fight for our heart

and those of our family, it's imperative that we learn how to guard our hearts from sinful appetites.

It's a fundamental truth that we are most vulnerable to sin during periods of emotional or physical pain. If you're bored, depressed, discouraged, or just tired, you'll likely look for something to create a mood swing—something to make you feel better. It's at just such times that the spiritual battle is intense and you need a strategy that will enable you to fight through the pain like one of David's mighty men did during an ancient battle.

A MAN WHO REFUSED TO RUN

A real fight isn't TaeBo. It's not like hitting one of those four-foot-tall inflatable punching bags that looks like a clown and makes a weak punch look like a Mike Tyson haymaker. If an unprepared boxer steps into a ring and fights for only three minutes, his arms and legs will turn into wet noodles. To keep that from happening, boxers train endlessly. They run for miles every day. They spar against tough opponents and relentlessly beat on a punching bag.

> **If we're going to win the war for our heart, we must understand our pain and have a strategy to fight through it effectively.**

The battle described in 2 Samuel 23:9-10 wasn't a ten-round bout—there was no bell at the end of three minutes so everyone could rest. The Israelites and Philistines were fighting each other with swords and spears. Sensing the tide turning against them, the Israelites retreated. But one man, Eleazar, refused to run. Gripping his sword,

he swung it like a wild, mechanical man—
left and right and up and down. The enemy
continued to advance, and he continued to
cut them down.

> **When a crisis hits, we're tempted to ignore the pain, stuff it, or deaden it. Instead, we must face the pain, understand it, and fight through it.**

Eleazar's legs and arms burned as lactic
acid rushed through his veins. The biblical
text says his "hand grew tired and froze to
the sword" (2 Samuel 23:10). His courage and
strength rallied the rest of the people, who
followed him and gathered plunder from
the fallen army.

Unlike the rest of the men engaged in
the battle, Eleazar didn't retreat. He refused to listen to his
fear and pain. Instead, he fought through them. I'm convinced if we're going to win the war for our heart, we must
understand our pain and have a strategy to fight through it
effectively.

FACE YOUR PAIN

As we pass through life, we are bound to face numerous
crises when we feel separated from something we value. It's
then that we realize we do not in fact have muscle power,
political power, sexual power (potency), relational power,
financial power, the power of knowledge, the power of
positive thinking, or personal power.[1] These kinds of losses
expose our weakness, and cause immense emotional pain.

When a crisis hits, we must enter into a deeper relationship with ourselves and with God. We're tempted to ignore
the pain, stuff it, or deaden it (with alcohol, drugs, sex,

food, work). Instead, we must face the pain, understand it, and fight through it.

In the legend of the quest for the Holy Grail, the classical tale of male heroism, we're told that when the Knights of the Round Table set out, each one entered a forest at the darkest place and forged a path where none had been before. Masculine strength is realized only when we find a path from emotional darkness to light. Your journey, like that of the Knights of the Round Table, is uniquely yours.

Along the way, you may get lost. The old Boy Scout manual offered good advice for those who get lost in the woods:

1. Don't panic.
2. Stop doing what you were doing.
3. Sit down and calm yourself.
4. Look for landmarks.
5. Follow trails.

Reflect on the first three steps for a moment—they're crucial. Once you've taken them, consider the following landmarks. They're intended to help you identify and understand your pain so you can face it and find your way to strength.

Landmark One: Lost Opportunities

The great English playwright and poet William Shakespeare described strategic moments that must be seized:

There is a tide in the affairs of men
Which, taken at the flood, leads on to fortune;
Omitted, all the voyage of their life
Is bound in shallows and in miseries.
On such a full sea are we now afloat,
And we must take the current when it serves,
Or lose our ventures.[2]

In the ancient world, ships would enter a harbor at high tide and receive cargo. Once loaded, a heavy vessel couldn't depart until the next high tide. If the captain failed to set sail during the high tide, he would miss the chance to leave port. Similarly, through the course of life, each of us encounters "strategic opportunities" that we must seize or forfeit forever.

When we seize such opportunities we reap the benefits. When we miss them, we suffer the losses. The Bible is filled with stories of men who failed to capitalize on a strategic opportunity.

When Abraham slept with Hagar he lost the chance to trust God and father his first son with Sarah.

Barak forfeited the right to be seen as a great leader when he asked Deborah to go to battle with him. His army won the battle, but a woman received the credit.

Esau lost his inheritance when he sold his birthright to Jacob for some stew and bread.

Moses forfeited an opportunity to enter the Promised Land when he struck the rock twice with his staff to bring forth water instead of speaking to it as God had commanded.

Samuel, Samson, and Peter also forfeited opportunities that cost them dearly.

You may have too. Maybe you failed to seize a financial opportunity because, like a lottery ticket, it seemed an unlikely winner. It could be you failed to apply yourself at work and it cost you a job you wish you still had. Maybe you made a poor strategic decision and it cost your company dearly. Perhaps more effort on your part would have nourished your marriage and prevented a divorce. That lost opportunity may be a source of ongoing pain.

Sometimes the missed opportunities we grieve center on a loss of youth. Maybe it was the chance to play a sport or date a girl. Maybe it was an opportunity to pursue a dream career or buy a home. Some of the opportunities we miss change the course of our lives. Others are mere bumps in the road. But they create pain, and sometimes it's intense.

Landmark Two: Lost Relationships

If we live long enough, all of us will suffer the loss of loved ones. Sometimes they're taken by death, like my little sister, Beckie, who died after a valiant fifteen-year battle with cancer.

Other times the relationship dies due to inattention or an event that irreparably damages it. Inattention acts like a slow leak—imperceptibly deflating the relationship, like a tiny hole in a tire, until it's void of affection. The event may have been an argument in which harsh words flew like a gunslinger's bullets, ripping the combatants to shreds. The most common casualties are wives, children, business

associates, or long-term friends. The emotional pain often proves unbearable and frequently results in depression.

If you initiated the relational loss, it's likely you later engaged in self-punishing thoughts and acts of retribution to assuage your guilt for having been the villain. "I blew it!" you may say. You may regret that you didn't honor your wife or spend time with your kids. You may offer gifts or money in an attempt to buy back their affection. Or you may engage in humiliating acts, like a beggar, to win back your wife, children, or friend. I know a man who repeatedly called his wife in tears begging her to forgive his past neglect. Instead of winning his wife back, his behavior repelled her.

If the other party triggered the breach you may be equally immersed in anger. You may wonder how he or she could have done or said such a thing. Your sense of justice may prevent you from seeking to bridge the gap. *He doesn't deserve my friendship,* you tell yourself. Even more harmful, you may hide behind an ever-growing barrier of isolation. Like a soldier in a battle tank, you close the hatch and hope the armor plating will protect you from harm.

We've all suffered the loss of relationships. And the pain often lingers for years, if not a lifetime.

Landmark Three: Lost Significance

As boys we dream of conquering the world. By adulthood we put away childish things and assume the role of provider, husband, and father. But we still retain a hope that success will come our way. Unfortunately, as we mature we compare our achievements to other men our age or younger.

I find it interesting that we seldom compare ourselves to men we think are below us on the achievement food chain. We always compare ourselves to those we believe have accomplished more than we have. We look to men who make more money, live in larger homes, or occupy corner offices on the top floor of a high-rise building. Compared to them we feel like failures. It seldom crosses our mind that those we envy are unfavorably comparing themselves to someone else.

I dislike this about myself. God has blessed me with a wonderful family, years of effective ministry, close friends, and published books. When I compare myself to men with larger ministries, greater influence, and better-selling books I feel insignificant. At such times I feel like a sailor trying to catch wind in my fluttering sails while other clippers glide past me. Such a distorted view of reality creates a deep and lingering sorrow.

My experience gives credence to the widely held belief that man's greatest need is significance. Solomon said that God has set eternity in the hearts of men (Ecclesiastes 3:11). Victor Frankl wrote, "Man's search for meaning is the chief motivation of his life." Patrick Morley observed that at one time or another we've all said:

"I want to have an impact."

"I want to make a difference."

"I want my life to have meaning."[3]

We strive for significance. When we realize we may never achieve all we once dreamed of accomplishing, we feel an unrelenting pain. We feel invisible and sense the

world is walking past without seeing us. Because we haven't been trained in how to cope with pain, we do what we can to ignore or deaden it.

WHY LIFE'S DIFFICULT

What makes life difficult isn't that we experience pain. It's made difficult by our passivity, which undermines our willingness to fight through pain. It prompts us to run away or try to deaden the pain in harmful ways. The faster we run away and the harder we work at killing the pain, the more our problems grow. We must slam on the brakes, throw away the anesthetic, and say we will run no more. Like Eleazar, we must fight through the pain instead of avoiding it.

In the battle for our heart and those of our family, it's essential that we implement a strategy that will enable us to cope with pain as mighty men, not cowards. The next time you're tempted to deaden your pain, stop and remember the three landmarks that cause pain. Ask yourself, *Why am I hurting?*

> What makes life difficult isn't that we experience pain. It's made difficult by our passivity, which undermines our willingness to fight through pain.

If it's due to a lost opportunity, then look ahead, not back. Follow Paul's example when he said, "Friends, don't get me wrong: By no means do I count myself an expert in all of this, but I've got my eye on the goal, where God is beckoning us onward— to Jesus. I'm off and running, and I'm not turning back" (Philippians 3:13-14, *The Message*).

If you're hurting due to a lost relationship, see a

counselor or your pastor about how to process the loss or pursue reconciliation. Seek God's comfort as David did when he penned the Twenty-third Psalm and spoke of God as the Shepherd who cares for, comforts, and protects his people.

If the pain is caused by a loss of significance, focus your attention on who you are and what you have through your relationship with Christ. Paul urged his readers to do this when he said, "God's Spirit touches our spirits and confirms who we really are. We know who he is, and we know who we are: Father and children. And we know we are going to get what's coming to us—an unbelievable inheritance! We go through exactly what Christ goes through. If we go through the hard times with him, then we're certainly going to go through the good times with him!" (Romans 8:16-17, *The Message*).

Please don't misunderstand me. My intention isn't to offer you a quick insight that will make your pain disappear like a card up a magician's sleeve. I simply want to mention landmarks that have helped me understand where I am and why I'm experiencing pain.

But often times the pain persists. On those occasions you must think through what caused your pain and then consider if relieving the pain through sinful actions will replace the loss. Of course it won't. That means you need a way of fighting through the pain that will enable you to avoid sinning and making things worse. You need a strategy that will be consistent with your identity as a warrior, your relationship with a holy God, and your role as the defender

of your family. You need a strategy that will show you how to fight for endurance by fighting through pain.

I want to offer you that strategy in the form of a trail for you to follow. It's a proven path that will get you to safety and enable you to resist the temptation to anesthetize your pain in a sinful way. Just as Eleazar had to exercise discipline to fight through his pain, so must you. If you don't, it's unlikely your wife or children will. The sins of the father are passed down from one generation to the next . . . as are his strengths.

THE BATTLE WITHIN

We must never lose sight of the fact that we're involved in spiritual warfare. Paul told the Galatians, "For the flesh sets its desire against the Spirit, and the Spirit against the flesh; for these are in opposition to one another, so that you may not do the things that you please" (Galatians 5:17, NASB).

Paul's words capture the essence of the internal battle being waged within each of us. In chapter nine we'll see how our victory is assured by God's Spirit. And we'll learn how to allow Christ to live through us in the power of the Spirit. The mighty men exhibited this sort of faith as well. Ultimately, Eleazar experienced victory because of his faith in God—not because of the strength of his arm or the edge of his sword. We're told in 2 Samuel 23:10 that "the Lord gave him a great victory

We're fighting an enemy who may customize the specifics of his approach but who never varies his basic attack.

that day" (NLT). Remember, the battle is spiritual. Never forget this truth.

But for now we need to recognize the fact that Satan works in conjunction with our flesh (the sinful desires that reside in us) to prompt us to cope with pain by gratifying our evil desires. We hear the whispers in our ear, promising to replace our suffering with pleasure. The process by which we're tempted always follows the same cycle. Please take a moment to contemplate this truth. We're fighting an enemy who may customize the specifics of his approach but who never varies his basic attack.

> Satan works in conjunction with our flesh (the sinful desires that reside in us) to prompt us to cope with pain by gratifying our evil desires.

Most of us fail to realize this and so we're overpowered time and again. We repeatedly commit the same sins. It's like the sign on an Alaskan highway: "Choose your rut carefully. You'll be in it for the next two hundred miles."

Of course, we don't have to fall into a rut. As warriors we can see it approaching and avoid it. Jesus summarized the process we follow when he said, "The good man brings good things out of the good stored up in him, and the evil man brings evil things out of the evil stored up in him" (Matthew 12:35).

The process is straightforward, isn't it? Sinful actions begin with sinful thoughts. One thing I admire about Jesus' teaching is that he breaks complex problems down to their simplest elements. What could be simpler: Bad behavior

follows bad thinking like stink follows a garbage truck. We fantasize about something sensual or self-serving that promises pleasure—and then we act.

David, the leader of the mighty men, learned this lesson too late. At the peak of his military prowess, after he had become king, he decided to stay in Jerusalem rather than join his troops in battle. Big mistake. The biblical text tells us, "One evening David got up from his bed and walked around on the roof of the palace. From the roof he saw a woman bathing. The woman was very beautiful" (2 Samuel 11:2).

Those three sentences trigger a series of questions. Had he seen the woman before? Is that why he stayed home from the battle? How long did he bask in her beauty? Now remember, we're talking about King David. It was God who said, "'I have found David son of Jesse a man after my own heart; he will do *everything* I want him to do'" (Acts 13:22; italics mine).

If David, the leader of the mighty men, could fall, it would be wise for us not to consider ourselves exempt. We need to understand the nature of temptation so we can resist it. While David serves as a warning, James, the half-brother of Jesus, provides us with insight into temptation. No doubt James must have learned a lot as he grew up with Jesus. Perhaps that's why he amplified Jesus' teachings with the words, "Each one is tempted when, by his own evil desire, he is dragged away and enticed. Then, after desire has conceived, it gives birth to sin; and sin, when it is full-grown, gives birth to death" (James 1:14-15). Notice the cycle in the graph on the following page:[4]

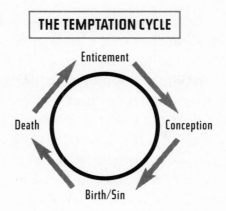

THE TEMPTATION CYCLE

Enticement

Death

Conception

Birth/Sin

Stage One: Enticement—The Flesh Is Aroused

During a time of pain caused by one of the landmarks (lost opportunities, lost relationships, or lost significance) our flesh—that part of our personality that craves gratification apart from God—will seek relief and remind us of a past pleasurable experience. We will begin thinking about a substance or behavior that promises not only relief but a positive mood swing as well. It may be something as harmless as a delicious dessert or as dangerous as a line of cocaine. Most of us live somewhere between these extremes. The more we think about the temptation, the more we want to act.

The word James used to describe this stage was *enticement*. The imagery is of a worm on a hook falling in front of a trout and drawing it out of its hiding place. Like that trout, our flesh may be hiding when the evil one drops a tantalizing temptation in our line of vision. Suddenly, a single thought draws our flesh to the bait and the hook it

hides. The thought then enters our consciousness, where it seeks to control our mind and will.

I realize nobody knows how David ended up in such a vulnerable situation. But I suspect his stroll on the roof of the palace wasn't a one-time event. In light of his devotion to God, I don't think a single glance at Bathsheba would have led to David's downfall. I believe that before her husband left for battle, the king had noticed her beauty. I suspect he had spent hours battling his sexual fantasies.

Why do I think this? Because few godly men quickly make the moral leap from seeing a naked woman to seducing her. Such an act, for a man of God, takes time. That's why it's crucial we break the cycle at the first stage—before desire can take root in our heart. No wonder Solomon said, "Above all else, guard your heart, for it is the wellspring of life" (Proverbs 4:23).

As spiritual warriors, we know the battlefield is our mind. It's a fertile field with a steel gate that we alone can guard. We must limit what enters through our eyes and ears. We must fortify our thoughts with Scripture and other healthy images. I'm convinced that's why Paul said, "Finally, brethren, whatever is true, whatever is honorable, whatever is right, whatever is pure, whatever is lovely, whatever is of good repute, if there is any excellence and if anything worthy of praise, let your mind dwell on these things" (Philippians 4:8, NASB).

> It's crucial that we break the cycle at the first stage—before desire can take root in our heart.

Stage Two: Conception—The Will Is Activated

Because we're not conditioned to "dwell on these things," we often surrender to the thoughts emanating from the flesh. The more we think about the pleasure it promises, the more we want to act. But instead of leaping from the thought to the act in a single big step, we take a small step . . . or a series of small steps. I've often said, "I'm one small step away from the first step in a series of steps that could lead to my ruin." I'm convinced David repeatedly strolled on the roof of his house hoping to see Bathsheba. The more he gazed at her flawless body, the more he wanted to possess it. That's true of us all. We take small steps, and these small steps take us into stage two of the temptation cycle: conception.

James has changed metaphors and is now referring to the birth process: "after desire has conceived." The seed of sin has been planted. Like a man with a pregnant wife, we anticipate the imminent delivery—in this case, of the sinful act. While we haven't given birth to the deed, we've engaged our will and we're carrying out what psychologists call the "rituals" that precede a sinful act.

A ritual is a practice or pattern of behavior regularly performed in a set manner. We tend to ritualize those behaviors that excite us. Nothing is more important for a man who wants to win the battle for his heart than identifying the rituals that precede an episode of acting out sin. While I realize your primary struggle may not be with sexual lust, I'm going to use that as an example because it's the biggest battle most men face. Some of the rituals men have mentioned to me include:

- Eyeing erotic images in video stores
- Driving though a red-light district
- Flirting with a coworker
- Watching pay-per-view movie previews in a hotel
- Calling a 900-number just to find out the price of a call
- Checking out personal ads in the newspaper

Each of us has unique rituals. Winning the battle for your heart demands that you eliminate every one.

To do so, make a list of the rituals that lead to your destructive behavior. It's probably not difficult for you to identify them. Think about the last time you fell in your area of greatest weakness and identify the behavior that preceded your fall. Once the list is made, define what you must do to eliminate each ritual and then discard it like radioactive waste.

We're all one small step away from the first step in a series of steps that could lead to our ruin.

I learned several years ago that without accountability, I'm as safe surfing the Web as a peg-legged man in a forest fire. Last year I signed up with a company called Covenant Eyes.* This Internet company keeps a non-erasable history of every Web site I visit and then e-mails it to two accountability partners of my choosing. One of my accountability partners is my twenty-one-year-old son. I can assure you that knowing my son will see every site I visit on the Internet harnesses my lust.

*For more information about Covenant Eyes, go to www.millionmightymen.com and click on the Covenant Eyes tab, or visit www.covenanteyes.com.

Such steps are necessary. When Jesus taught us to pray by saying, "And lead us not into temptation, but deliver us from the evil one" (Matthew 6:13), he didn't mean to imply that God could or would lead us into temptation. Instead, he wanted us to ask God to never allow us to have the inclination to sin when we have the opportunity. Why? Because when inclination and opportunity come together, we'll probably sin.

I've learned that while I can't always control my desires, I can usually control my environment. I can protect myself from temptation by eliminating rituals. We live in a culture that provides us ample avenues to sin. Our responsibility is to create an environment that is as spiritually safe as possible.

Here's an example. Remember my story at the beginning of the chapter about the naked girl next door? After discovering that two men in my small group had struggled with voyeurism for a couple of years, I decided to take aggressive action to protect myself. I visited my neighbor, whom I had never met. Without incriminating myself, I urged him to keep his shades down at night so that nobody could use my yard as a platform to invade his privacy.

He thanked me and said that a few weeks earlier his teenage daughter had actually seen a man peering through one of their windows. When she opened the door he jumped over the fence and fled through my backyard.

A few weeks later, while turning on my sprinkler system late one night, I noticed that the shades to his house were

down. Yes, I looked again. And I looked hoping the shades would be up and the light on. But because I had taken decisive action during a time of strength, I protected myself from temptation during a moment of weakness.

Once you do this you'll hear your flesh begging for a different ritual that will lead to sensual gratification. If you ignore such pleadings the pain you were trying to deaden may intensify. At just such times you must remember that God's purpose for emotional pain is to strengthen you. Visualize yourself as a mighty man standing your ground and fighting for control of your heart. Fight the pain caused by one of the landmarks and determine that you will not surrender your heart to the pain. Recognize that rituals are enemy scouts that want to sneak past the gate and prepare a way for the main force. The victory is yours, but you must keep watch over the gate to your heart.

Stage Three: Birth—The Sin Is Committed

Birth naturally follows conception. If we allow ourselves to get to stage two, the act that has been dreamed about and planned is finally carried out. The tantalizing bait is tasted. For David that meant summoning beautiful Bathsheba to his room. For you it means—well, only you know what it means for you. Ultimately, after the sin is committed we dangle like a fish on a hook. The pleasure of the bait is gone. All that remains is the tear in our heart and the sharp and enduring pain of the hook.

Stage Four: Death—The Relationship with God and Others Is Lost

David, one of the godliest men in the Old Testament, committed murder to cover his sin. (We'll look at this in the next chapter.) Filled with shame and despair, he ran from God for a year. Later his beloved son Absalom publicly seduced the king's wives on the roof of the palace. What David had done in private, Absalom did in public. The night David surrendered his heart to the enemy, he also endangered Absalom's heart. While he found God's forgiveness, he also suffered the consequences of his sin. We always do. And so does our family.

Fortunately, we don't have to sin. We don't have to allow our pain to drive us off the ground we're protecting. We can break the temptation cycle and win the battle for our heart.

We need to commit to fortifying our minds with the Bible and positive thoughts. We must identify every dangerous ritual and ruthlessly destroy it. But even that won't be enough. We'll never win the battle for our heart alone. Like David, we need other mighty men to provide us with support and encouragement. A passive man will never develop these kinds of friends. The only men with such devoted buddies are men who engage in the fifth battle and fight for their friends. In the next chapter you'll discover how you can become a warrior who never leaves a friend behind.

Discussion Questions

1. Why do Christian men tend to hide behind a mask of spirituality?

2. Which of the three landmarks causes you the most pain? Why?

3. What harmful actions or things do you use to deaden emotional pain?

4. When Jesus urged us to ask the Father to never lead us into temptation, what did he mean? Why is this so important?

5. What rituals do you need to remove from your life when you're strong in order to protect yourself when you're weak?

6. Why is it so important in the battle for our heart that we have a battle plan to help us fight through pain? What's your plan?

BATTLE FIVE

Fight for Your Friends

A compelling scene from a nature show airing on *Animal Planet* shows a herd of gazelles grazing in the middle of a meadow. The golden grass is two, maybe three, feet tall. The sky is heavy and gray, with hot clouds hanging like tattered sheets. The graceful gazelles with their ringed horns that curve backward and inward are focused on the grass, not on the danger that lurks close by.

In the foreground a leopard creeps slowly from the left to the right of the screen. A soft breeze blows the grass back and forth in front of the leopard, his camouflage coat rendering him almost invisible. He stops and gazes at the herd.

A single gazelle, savoring the sweet grass, forgets the herd and the safety it offers. He stands alone, head down, eating.

The leopard locks his eyes on the lone gazelle.

He stiffens—like a statue.

He attacks.

The gazelle springs into the air. He darts to the right. He cuts to the left. The leopard runs as fast as the wind. He closes in on his prey. He lashes out with his right paw and hits the rear legs of the gazelle, knocking it to the ground.

In an instant, the leopard clamps his jaws on the gazelle's throat.

The graceful gazelle lies motionless. His brown eyes dart about. In a few moments he will be dead. Why? Because he wandered from the herd. He could have been the slowest, smallest, and weakest gazelle in the meadow, but if he had stayed in the middle of the herd, he would have been safe. Each time I watch that clip I'm moved by the cruelty of the leopard and the weakness of the gazelle.

> **We must learn a lesson from the gazelle and stay close to the herd. Alone, we're weak. Together, we're strong.**

As a scuba diver I frequently see large schools of fish. Like the gazelle, they find safety in numbers. It's instinctive—God programmed them this way. We humans lack such instincts—but we face a greater danger.

Peter said, "Your enemy the devil prowls around like a roaring lion looking for someone to devour" (1 Peter 5:8). Hidden from our view, the devil stalks us. He watches to see when we're alone, weak, and vulnerable. Then he attacks.

A LESSON FROM THE GAZELLE

We must learn a lesson from the gazelle and stay close to the herd. Alone, we're weak. Together, we're strong. To be-

come effective warriors, we must learn to stick together and fight for our friends.

I've thought long and hard about this chapter. I've asked myself: *Why are you writing it? What effect do you want it to have on the men who read it?* The answer is simple, really. I hope it enables you to see your need for close friends. But more than that, I hope it prompts you to offer God's strength to other men, and in the process, find it for yourself. David found this type of strength in three of his mighty men.

David hadn't yet ascended to the throne of Israel. Instead of ruling a nation, he was leading a ragtag band of warriors who lived like refugees. At one point, while David was hiding in a limestone cave on the face of a cliff, the black snake of despair uncoiled in his gut. His situation seemed hopeless. No wonder—a Philistine army waited below. He felt like a trapped animal.

As men we fear losing our independence. We fear anything that, like paralysis, threatens our mobility by robbing us of power, control, and the ability to realize our dreams. When our worst fear materializes, we realize how isolated we are and we feel a deep sense of loneliness. At such times we enter a dark pit of despair that reeks of death. We wonder why we are here and why we should keep living.

While struggling with such feelings David remembered the well he drank from as a boy in Bethlehem. He longed for a cup of water from that well. He ached for the freedom he knew as a child. He feared he would never taste that water because the Philistines blocked the way. Like a man

serving a life sentence behind bars, he had no hope for the future.

David wasn't alone in the cave. His mighty men stood nearby. Three of them saw his despair. They heard him utter, "Oh, that someone would get me a drink of water from the well near the gate of Bethlehem" (2 Samuel 23:15). A moment later they departed with no more sound than the night makes when it turns to day.

What happened next amazes me. These three men broke through the Philistine lines like a 250-pound NFL running back romping through a Pop Warner team. They got to the well in Bethlehem, drew water from it, and fought through enemy lines again to return to David.

It would be easy to conclude from that story that David lacked water in his cave hideout. In reality, it wasn't merely water he lacked but *hope*. He had experienced every landmark: David likely felt as though he had lost his opportunity to be the king; he had lost his relationship with Saul and Saul's son, Jonathan; and he probably felt a loss of significance as he scurried around the desert without so much as a home. He may have felt like:

A husband whose unfaithful wife has a faraway look in her eyes.

A father whose dying child gasps for breath.

An executive whose failing company can't get another loan.

An unemployed man whose best job lead called and said, "Not now."

A recovering alcoholic who just spent his last dollar on a bottle of cheap wine.

A man whose fiancée returned the ring and said, "Let's just be friends."

By breaking through enemy lines, the three men offered David hope. They proved he wasn't trapped. They demonstrated that the enemy could be outsmarted and overpowered.

When they returned with the water, David said it represented their blood, which they had eagerly risked for him. He considered it too precious a gift for him to drink, so he poured the water onto the ground as an offering to God and an act of thanksgiving for preserving their lives (2 Samuel 23:16-17).

> A sacrificial act of friendship honors God like few things a man can do.

On the surface such an act seems to minimize their heroic deed. After all, the men had risked everything, and David showed his gratitude not only by refusing to drink the water but by pouring it onto the ground. I can assure you that those three men didn't see it that way. On the contrary, as David emptied the cup, their hearts filled with a pure love for their leader.

He elevated their heroic act to a deed so sacrificial, so loving, and so brave that he would not defile it by drinking

the water. David's response bears testimony to the fact that a sacrificial act of friendship honors God like few things a man can do. I suspect the three mighty men were awed by the honor David showed them. Seeking to serve, they were served. Seeking to lift up their friend, they were lifted up.

Such friendship evades most men. We need friends who understand our fears and offer us protection, men who will stand guard around us during our times of vulnerability and shame.

It's unfortunate that so many men never allow others to shelter them and stand guard for them. Because most men steer clear of close relationships, they never connect with men who will help them in that way. As I've talked with guys, I've discovered that most feel their struggles are personal . . . private . . . and sometimes shameful. It's not the sort of thing they want other men to see.

Yet I'm convinced we all need a few close friends. Men who understand our struggles and provide us with protection and encouragement. Men who will be there during our darkest night and hardest battle.

THREE FRIENDSHIP TRAITS

How can you have friends like the three mighty men who got the cup of water for David? Equally important, how can you be such a friend yourself? I've identified three traits that characterized David's mighty men. Each is crucial.

Friendship Trait #1: Focused Listener

My favorite *Far Side* cartoon shows a dog leaning out the

back window of a car as it drives past a house. The dog spots a canine friend in the front yard of the house and shouts at him, "Ha ha ha, Biff. Guess what? After we go to the post office, I'm going to the vet's to be *tutored!*"

That poor dog is about to find out that he didn't listen very well. That's something we're all guilty of. I've often wondered why we men find it so hard to listen at an emotional level. Why do we often hear only the words someone speaks without perceiving the emotions and deeper meaning behind the words? I think I know the answer, but I don't think you'll like it—I know I don't.

> Listening requires time and effort. It demands that you consistently remind yourself to focus on your friend's needs, not yours.

Most men feel more comfortable with their dog, if they have one, than they do with other men. They feed it, bathe it, pet it, cuddle it, and, like the driver in the *Far Side* cartoon, let it ride in their car with its head hanging out the passenger window. They even talk to their dog.

In his book *The Road Less Traveled,* Dr. M. Scott Peck observed several reasons why men attach themselves so closely to a pet.

First, they don't know what their pet is thinking—if it's thinking at all. Consequently, they project their own thoughts and feelings onto their pet.

Second, they enjoy their pet only insofar as the animal's will corresponds to their own. Most men won't keep a pet very long if it consistently fights against them.

Finally, men foster the pet's dependency on them. Men crave this because it makes them feel needed.

Sadly, many men are only capable of loving pets and are incapable of loving other people.[1] Why? I suspect it's because they don't know how to interact on an intellectual and emotional level with another person. They don't know how to escape the gravitational pull of their own thoughts and feelings and enter into the orbit of another man. They're comfortable as long as the relationship, like a pet, affirms much and demands little.

Deep and enduring friendships require self-sacrifice that's driven by love. Unfortunately, we men aren't used to using the word *love* when speaking of our feelings for another man. Yet Jesus never hesitated to use the word. On the night before his death, Christ repeatedly spoke of his love for the disciples. He said, "Just as the Father has loved Me, I have also loved you" (John 15:9, NASB).

The three men who risked their lives for David loved him. They heard words he spoke in a whisper. Had they not understood the message behind what he said, they might have handed him a cup of water from the reserve in the cave. Instead, they saw his real need and met it.

I don't score too high on listening tests. The problem isn't with my ears—I can hear very well. My problem is that I'm focused on educating or impressing rather than understanding. Or else I pretend to listen while my mind is somewhere else. I've caught myself listening to a friend pour out his heart on the phone while I focus on a football game I'm watching on a muted television set. I'm like a dog

that can hear a package of food being opened half a block away yet not hear someone talking at his side.

Listening intently requires breaking away from self-absorption and tuning in, not only to the spoken words of a friend but also to the meaning behind those words. It involves listening to the tone of his voice, reading his body language, and knowing the meaning of his silence.

One of my close friends clams up when he's processing something. His silence means he needs space. Like a rubber band, he pulls away only to return. If I go after him and try to pull out his thoughts too soon, it annoys him. I've learned to listen by waiting for him to process information and then let me know when he wants to talk. Another buddy is just the opposite. When he stops talking he needs me to pursue him and find out what's happening.

Listening requires time and effort. It demands that you consistently remind yourself to focus on your friend's needs, not yours. Sure, we can all love a pet—it demands nothing in return. Loving other men requires an act of God's grace in our life that produces love and prompts self-sacrifice.

Once you've truly listened to a friend, you'll want to take the next step.

Friendship Trait #2: Big League Encourager

It's crucial that we learn to listen, because listening fosters empathy. And empathy marks the character of a man who has escaped self-absorption. No longer is he preoccupied with money, power, reputation, health, and pleasure. He understands his own wounds, and as he listens to a friend

he understands his pain. He feels his friend's agony as if it were his own.

No longer is there a need to one-up each other, or to interrupt. Instead the driving desire is to listen and understand—from such understanding flows encouragement. It's important to realize that encouragement takes many forms. It may consist of a courageous act like pursuing a friend even in the face of rejection, speaking optimistic words, offering a spiritual perspective, or spending quality time.

The cup of water the mighty men offered David assured him, "You're not trapped. You're not helpless. You're not beaten. You're not alone." It filled him with courage—which is what the word *encouragement* means.

> The cup of water the mighty men offered David assured him, "You're not trapped. You're not helpless. You're not beaten. You're not alone."

Several years ago I faced a life-changing crisis exacerbated by events beyond my control. While I was talking with a friend on the phone he said, "I'll pick you up in the morning, and we'll spend the day together."

"But I thought you had to fly to San Diego to close a deal," I replied.

"I did. But not anymore," he said. "Now I need to be here for you." My friend listened, entered into my suffering, and infused me with courage.

Although Jonathan isn't listed among David's mighty men, he certainly proved himself valiant in battle and loyal in friendship. At a time when David faced

daily danger, Jonathan encouraged him in two ways. First, he ran interference for him. When Jonathan's father, King Saul, sought to kill David, the young prince spoke with his father about David's innocence and later helped David escape the king's wrath (1 Samuel 19:1-7; 20:1-42).

Second, he reminded David of God's promises. Exhausted by King Saul's relentless pursuit, the giant-killer despaired. Seeking refuge, David and his band of men hid in a cave in the desert hills of Ziph. Jonathan knew his friend suffered from deep depression. And he knew his hiding place. Disregarding the wrath of his father, Jonathan found David and offered him hope. The prince told his friend, "Don't be afraid. . . . My father Saul will not lay a hand on you. You will be king over Israel, and I will be second to you. Even my father Saul knows this" (1 Samuel 23:17).

That brief encounter was the last time David would see his friend alive. But what an encounter! Jonathan reminded David that God would one day make him king. In this affirmation, Jonathan acknowledged that even though he was the king's son, David would sit on the throne. Jonathan's devotion to David washed away any sense of competition or jealousy and enabled him to encourage his friend.

Every warrior suffers setbacks and encounters pain. During those dark nights we need a friend with a light to show us the way . . . a friend who will listen to us and encourage us. And we need to be such a friend to others. By now you may realize that such friendship often involves the next trait . . . taking risks.

Friendship Trait #3: Courageous Risk Taker

Risk taking is something we do every day. Of the thousands or millions of risks we take in a lifetime, the most significant are those involved in loving other people. When we take such risks, we make ourselves vulnerable to betrayal and rejection.

Self-absorption and passivity restrict our ability to take relational risks. They keep us from sharing openly with another man about our fears, disappointments, and failures. They prevent us from listening to another man's fears or challenging his thinking or behavior when we see he's struggling. They bridle our willingness to enter into deep and lasting friendships. And they cost us dearly.

Consider the likelihood that David committed adultery in part because he had nobody to openly share his struggles and temptation with. Later, to cover his sin, the king had Bathsheba's husband, Uriah the Hittite, murdered. That ruthless act is made worse by the fact that Uriah was one of his mighty men—someone who had pledged to serve David and someone David had trusted with his life. (See 2 Samuel 23:39.) Could David have avoided both sins if he had had a few buddies with whom he could share his internal battles? I think so. I find it disheartening that a man who had such close friends while he ran from Saul isolated himself once he ascended to the throne. No longer did he enjoy the camaraderie of battle or the unity found around a fire at night. It saddens me that a man who demonstrated such boldness in battle lacked the courage to openly share the secrets of his private life.

Yet, both love and maturity demand risk taking. As boys we climbed on a bike one day and tried to ride it. While our dad held the bike upright we wobbled forward, afraid we would fall and skin our knees or break an arm. But we took the risk and eventually learned to keep our balance and ride. As we've grown up we've taken other risks—asking a girl out on a date, applying for a job, or buying a home.

As warriors we must realize that we cannot win the battle for our heart alone. We need other men and other men need us, just as David needed the three men who risked their lives to provide him with a cup of hope. Solomon realized this when he said, "Though one may be overpowered, two can defend themselves. A cord of three strands is not quickly broken" (Ecclesiastes 4:12).

> As warriors we must realize that we cannot win the battle for our heart alone. We need other men and other men need us.

I think most adult men lack close friends because they refuse to take the risks necessary for an enduring friendship. Herb Goldberg speaks of these risks in his book *The Hazards of Being Male,* in which he identifies the four phases of friendship. According to Goldberg, the highest form of friendship is "buddyship." While the word *buddy* isn't one that men use much anymore, Goldberg likes the term because it connotes youthfulness and spontaneity. He believes that this, when combined with adult maturity, contains the potential for the "ultimate masculine friendship."[2]

Men seldom reach the deepest phase of friendship

because it only comes after a crisis. Many of us remember as kids becoming closer buddies with a friend after a fistfight. Similarly, we become buddies with a man only after our friendship has survived a crisis that threatens to destroy the relationship.

The breach is frequently created by an act of insensitivity that inflicts deep pain. My friend Bob had heard for years about my insensitivity. We had even joked about it. One day, shortly after the death of his mother, he experienced it firsthand. My lack of compassion so deeply wounded him that he broke off communication with me for over a year. Finally, he contacted me. He came to the conclusion that he valued our friendship so much he was willing to run the risk that I might hurt him again.

On another occasion I had a falling out with a friend over money. His attitude hurt me so significantly I wasn't sure I wanted to continue the relationship. And then I reflected on the years of friendship we had enjoyed. I realized he had endured my weaknesses for years. I decided that no matter what he may have done to me or might do in the future, I loved him so much I would never give up on him. I would be his friend until death. I love that man!

Both of those relational crises revealed personal weaknesses and vulnerabilities in my friend or in me that hadn't been obvious before—even though we had known each other for years. In such cases both men are wounded and face the temptation to abandon the relationship. In fact, that seems like the easiest thing to do.

At this point the friendship stands on the brink of

destruction. The two men will both part and never be close again, or they'll repair the breach and become buddies. Growth in the relationship occurs when both men conclude that the friendship is more important than their wounds. It takes place when each sees the weakness in his friend and decides to stick with the friendship anyway.[3]

Entering into this phase of friendship requires taking a big risk. Specifically, *a man must risk suffering another wound at the hands of his friend*. Most men will simply walk away and say, "I don't need a friend like that."

We become like the lost Chihuahua featured in a cartoon. His owner, an extremely large man with a waist the size of a Volkswagen and buttocks that look like two oversized down pillows, pins a picture of the lost dog on a bulletin board at the grocery store. The man hopes someone will find his lost companion. Meanwhile, the poor Chihuahua is seen lodged, face first, between the two pillows that fill the back of the man's trousers. While the cartoon evokes a laugh, it also demonstrates how those who love us the most often hurt us the most. Indeed, like the dog's master, even their attempts to help us sometimes create more pain because they don't know where we are. Nor do they understand our suffering or its source.

I suspect you can think of a close friend who has hurt you. The wrong may have involved money, loyalty, or insensitivity. Whatever the cause, it hurt and your friendship never recovered.

There could be hope for the recovery of this relationship if you were to say, "He hurt me. But I love him enough

that I'm willing to endure this weakness in his personality and continue to be his friend. I'm willing to run the risk that he'll hurt me again." Buddyship, like a nut in a shell, only comes out when it's cracked by a hard blow.

When you take this step, your friendship has the opportunity to enter a phase where you'll feel comfortable with each other when you're weak, acting foolish, or being vulnerable. You'll feel like brothers and will diligently look out for each other, protecting one another from exploitation.[4] You'll help one another win the battle for the heart. Once you have a buddy, you won't want to leave him behind. You'll make sure that you never abandon him when he's struggling. You'll endure his weaknesses, even when he hurts you. You'll ask tough questions and demand an explanation when you perceive ungodly attitudes and actions.

THE RANGER'S CREED

In a fast-paced, hard-driving TV commercial, the U.S. armed forces send a clear message to potential soldiers: "You do not leave a fallen comrade on the field of battle."

That creed was tested several years ago in Afghanistan when two huge MH-47 helicopters came under heavy fire from small arms and rocket-propelled grenades. A hydraulic line in one of the birds was cut, so the choppers veered away to the north, climbing steeply. When they finally set down they discovered the rear gunner on one of the helicopters, Navy SEAL Neil Roberts, was missing. He had apparently been jolted out when the chopper banked hard to the north.

The Rangers decided to risk their lives. They asked for and received permission to go after their man. A short time later, six commandos were dropped off to search for Roberts. It was not until midnight that the last U.S. soldier was evacuated. The choppers also carried eleven wounded and seven bodies—Roberts and his six would-be rescuers. Those six men died because they chose to risk their lives rather than leave one of their buddies behind.[5]

Once you have a buddy, you'll never allow him to be left behind.

Friendship seldom demands that we risk our physical lives. But like the Rangers, we must be willing to risk ourselves for the sake of a buddy. He must know we will never leave him behind—no matter the risk. And we must know with equal certainty that we'll never be left behind either.

LOCKING ARMS

When I'm delivering this message at men's events I always conclude by inviting the four largest men present to join me on the stage. I ask the behemoths to stand beside one another, and I then casually walk in front of the men and softly shove each one in the chest. Even a gentle shove pushes the men off balance and they take a step back to regain their balance.

I then ask the men to form a circle and lock arms. Once they're in this stance I use both hands, and one at a time, I ram each man hard in the center of his back. But because their arms are locked, they're as immovable as a wall.

As spiritual warriors we must lock arms by sharing our

struggles and vulnerabilities. It's the only way we'll be able to stand against the attacks of the enemy. And we must fight for our friends by laying down our self-interest and genuinely listening to them. We must engage with them even though we run the risk of getting hurt. We must learn a lesson from the gazelle and stay near the herd. Together we're strong. Alone we're weak.

Each of the five battles we've looked at so far will end in defeat if we aren't willing to engage in the final one. Ultimately, David's mighty men experienced victory because they fought for a strong faith in God. As you read the final chapter, you'll discover how you can fight for the kind of faith that will unleash God's power through you.

Discussion Questions

1. Why do men fear losing their independence?

2. In 2 Samuel 23:15, why did David long for water from the well in Bethlehem? What did he really need? Why?

3. Have there been times you lacked hope and needed a friend to listen? When?

4. How can you be a better listener?

5. What can you do to be a better encourager? For suggestions, review how Jonathan encouraged David.

6. Why do most men have few, if any, buddies?

7. What would you have to do to have a buddy? To be one?

8. Why is it important in the battle for your heart that you have a few close friends?

formula. But it's as hard to practice in the heat of a battle as it is to sink a winning free throw in the final second of a basketball game. Yet that's precisely what David's mighty men did. After Eleazar defeated the Philistines single-handedly we read, "The Lord brought about a great victory that day" (2 Samuel 23:10). Later, after Shammah successfully defended his field of beans we're told, "The Lord brought about a great victory" (2 Samuel 23:12). The Hebrew word used for "victory" speaks of deliverance or salvation brought about by God through a man. These men realized that if they were trying to honor God and were trusting in him, they would be supernaturally empowered. They knew no enemy could stand against such a man.

The same is true for us today. When we're fighting for what's important to God—including guarding our heart from the enemy—victory is ours for the taking if we rely on God's power. We have a daily opportunity to live like David's mighty men as we engage in spiritual combat and fight the sixth battle—the battle for a strong faith. Doing so demands we develop three faith builders that will root our manhood in the power of God.

FAITH BUILDER #1:
RELY ON GOD'S POWER IN CHRIST

When David called Shammah a mighty man, he changed his identity from *Waste* to *Warrior*. It's imperative that those of us who follow Jesus realize we are new men in Christ. Regardless of your background or past experiences, you are a new man if you have trusted Christ as your personal Savior.

Paul told the Galatians, "I have been crucified with Christ and I no longer live, but Christ lives in me" (Galatians 2:20).

The old Paul, all that he was before he met Christ, died on the cross. After his conversion he was a new person—united with Jesus in his resurrection.

God has left an intricate watermark on our life in the likeness of Christ.

In Romans 6:6-8 we're told, "For we know that our old self was crucified with him so that the body of sin might be done away with, that we should no longer be slaves to sin—because anyone who has died has been freed from sin. Now if we died with Christ, we believe that we will also live with him."

The single most important element in waging spiritual warfare rests in our identity in Christ. God has left an intricate watermark on our life in the likeness of Christ. Its unique design becomes visible when we put our faith in God. At that moment, the power of Christ and his unlimited strength propel us to victory.

You're a New Man

Because of that spiritual reality, we've been changed as radically as a caterpillar that has metamorphosed into a butterfly. This truth is crucial in combating the pressures in our culture that tempt us to base our identity on what we own and who we know. God says our significance isn't based on our income or influence. It's based on who we are in Jesus.

Everything flows from our new identity. God has called us to battle and equipped us to win. But the battle is spiritual.

A reservoir of God's power is available to us, but we must not sip it through a straw. The more deeply we drink from the life of Christ, the more we will experience victory in our daily life.

Who Can Bully Superman?

I've always believed that in a battle of superheroes, Superman would win hands down. He has more power than a locomotive, can fly faster than a speeding bullet, can see through objects, and has skin tougher than the armor plating of a tank. His only vulnerability is Kryptonite, fragments of his exploded home planet. Without Kryptonite, nobody could stop Superman.

Nobody, that is, except Superman. In the movie *Superman II*, the man of steel travels to an Arctic fortress where he willingly gives up his superpowers so he can live with a mortal, Lois Lane. On the return trip to Metropolis from the fortress, the couple stops at a diner to get a hot dog. Seating Lois at the end of the lunch counter, Clark Kent heads to the men's room. In his absence a local bully named Rocky takes Clark's seat.

Upon his return Clark challenges Rocky to a fight. "Would you like to step outside?" Clark asks.

"After you, Four-Eyes," Rocky says. As Clark turns to go outside, Rocky hammers him from behind. Bleeding, Clark falls to the floor. Lois kneels down to comfort him. A moment later Clark struggles to his feet with a new resolve; he attacks Rocky, who again knocks him to the floor.

My favorite scene in the movie occurs toward the end

when Clark, with renewed superpowers, returns to the diner and has a rematch with Rocky. While Clark looks the same on the outside, an inner change has occurred. Instead of intimidating Clark and beating him to a pulp, Rocky sits helplessly on a diner chair as Clark spins him around like the blades on a ceiling fan.

The fantasy of Superman illustrates the transformation that occurs when we trust Christ as our Savior. While we can't stop a train or fly faster than a speeding bullet, we do possess not only God's holiness but also his supernatural strength. The living God has taken up residence in us, delivering us from the power of sin and providing us with the strength we need to live victoriously. As long as we rely on Christ to live through us, our lives will express the character of God.

I'm confident that most of the men in ancient Israel knew about the power of God. Throughout their lives they had heard stories about how God led their people out of Egypt and into the Promised Land. They had seen God direct them. They even knew he had promised, "You will pursue your enemies, and they will fall by the sword before you. Five of you will chase a hundred, and a hundred of you will chase ten thousand, and your enemies will fall by the sword before you" (Leviticus 26:7-8).

In spite of the fact that *every* man in Israel during the time of David had access to that promise and could have been a channel for God's power, only a handful were mighty men. These few believed that God + Me = Victory. They relied on the strength of God and became conduits for his power.

They aren't the only ones. The Bible tells stories of other men who trusted in God and realized his power.

Moses trusted God and saw the Red Sea parted.

Joshua trusted God and saw the walls of Jericho collapse.

Samson, filled with God's Spirit, ripped apart a lion with his bare hands.

Elijah trusted God and saw a widow's son raised from the dead.

Paul trusted God and saw countless people brought to faith in Christ as a result of his preaching, even though he didn't consider himself a good speaker (see 1 Corinthians 2:3-5).

These men weren't great because they possessed superior intelligence or physical strength. They were great because they relied on God's power. That's something you and I can do every day of our lives. It doesn't necessarily mean we'll see God raise the dead or part the waters of a river, but it does mean we'll sense his power enabling us to live as the men he created us to be and to have a mighty role in God's work in the world.

Such a statement isn't wishful thinking. God has promised to unleash his strength through us. Before ascending to heaven Jesus said, "You will receive power when the Holy Spirit comes on you" (Acts 1:8).

As believers in Jesus we don't need to question if we have power. We have it. We don't need to wonder if God

> **While we can't stop a train or fly faster than a speeding bullet, we do possess not only God's holiness but also his supernatural strength.**

will give us victory. It's ours. When Clark Kent returned to the diner and confronted Rocky, he didn't need more strength. He just needed to use the strength residing within him. Similarly, we must trust Jesus to enable us to experience the power and victory we already possess in him. And remember, as we saw in chapter four, God's power is perfected in your weakness.

The next time you find yourself in spiritual combat, don't try to fight in your own strength. That's a formula for failure. You can no more defeat the evil one in your own power than you can weave a silk rope out of salt.

Instead, we can go to God and say, "Thank you for delivering me from my weakness. And thank you that the Holy Spirit now lives in me. Right now I'm trusting you to empower me to do what is right and to experience the victory I already have in you."

FAITH BUILDER #2: RELY ON GOD'S PRESENCE

I think one reason we fail to trust in God when we're tempted is because we can't see him. Since we can't see God, we try to *feel* the warm glow of his presence with outstretched emotional hands. And if we don't feel him, we falsely conclude he's not there. Or we think he's there but he's unavailable to help us.

At the same time, we *feel* our flesh pleading for sensual gratification, our despair begging for a crumb of hope, our pride craving vindication, and our bitterness seeking revenge.

Our problem is that we live in a three-dimensional

world and God lives in a parallel spiritual dimension. He is with us even though we can't see him or feel him—like ultraviolet rays or radio waves.

Astrophysicist Dr. Hugh Ross provides an excellent illustration. He suggests we imagine that the two-dimensional image on a television screen actually constitutes a two-dimensional world. If you placed your fingertip on the screen, what would the people in the two-dimensional world see? Your fingertip would be a flat, round, two-dimensional image that would look like a dot. No one in that world would be able to see or comprehend depth any more than a blind person could comprehend color.

> Our feelings are unreliable when it comes to sensing God's presence. He's there, but our spiritual antenna doesn't always receive the signal.

If you entered that two-dimensional world and told the people about the three-dimensional world outside of their own, some would believe. But nobody would possess depth perception. They would have to take the existence of such a world by faith.[1]

Similarly, God doesn't exist just on the other side of the galaxy. He is with us. On occasion he has made himself known through the appearance of angels, a message to the prophets, or, in the case of Moses, a burning bush. His greatest manifestation occurred when he actually became a man, Jesus Christ. John said that he and others saw Jesus with their eyes and touched him with their hands (1 John 1:1).

The challenge we face is believing in the presence of a God we can't see or touch. Jesus understood the difficulty

of such faith. After his resurrection Jesus told Thomas, "Because you have seen me, you have believed; blessed are those who have not seen and yet have believed" (John 20:29).

Occasionally we sense God's presence at a deep emotional level. But our feelings can't reliably detect God's presence. We're like an old black-and-white TV with damaged rabbit-ear antennas. Sometimes the reception is clear, but at other times all we see is an intermittent horizontal spin. In order to clear up the reception we'll occasionally move the antenna around. But even if we can't see the picture, the TV signal fills the room around the television set. Similarly, our feelings are unreliable when it comes to sensing God's presence. He's there, but our spiritual antenna doesn't always receive the signal.

I used to ask God to show himself to me visibly. He never did—at least not in the way I expected. I can't help but think my faith would be stronger if an angel, or angels, would appear to me as they did to Elisha's servant.

It's an impressive illustration of God's existence in a parallel dimension. We read in 2 Kings 6 that the king of Aram was engaged in a war with the king of Israel. After a series of military setbacks, the Aramean king discovered that God was revealing his battle plans to the prophet Elisha, and Elisha was passing them along to the king of Israel. Seeking to kill the prophet, the king sent an army to Dothan, Elisha's hometown.

When the prophet's servant awoke and went outside, he saw the city surrounded by an enemy army of horses and

chariots. Terrified, he asked his master, "What shall we do?" Not a bad question considering the apparent hopelessness of the situation.

The prophet calmly said, "Don't be afraid. Those who are with us are more than those who are with them" (2 Kings 6:16).

I don't think Elisha's servant bought into the prophet's evaluation. His twenty-twenty vision told him a massive army surrounded them. He may have rubbed his eyes and looked again, but the odds did not appear to be in their favor.

Sensing his servant's fear, Elisha prayed, "O Lord, open his eyes so he may see" (2 Kings 6:17). Immediately a miracle occurred. God allowed Elisha's servant to see into the spiritual dimension. The text says, "Then the Lord opened the servant's eyes, and he looked and saw the hills full of horses and chariots of fire all around Elisha" (2 Kings 6:17).

I wonder, *did Elisha see the angels all along, or did he simply believe they were there?* In either case, he lived with an acute awareness of God's presence. I believe if God "opened our eyes" so we could see into the parallel spiritual dimension, we would see the Holy Spirit, with a host of angels, always at our side.

Such a statement rests on biblical revelation. Jesus himself promised, "I will ask the Father, and he will give you another Counselor to be with you forever" (John 14:16). The author of Hebrews reminds us that God promised, "Never will I leave you; never will I forsake you" (Hebrews 13:5). Elsewhere he asks, "Are not all angels ministering spirits sent to serve those who will inherit salvation?" (Hebrews 1:14).

The source of your spiritual power isn't across the room, down the street, or on the other side of town. He is within you and beside you. He is closer than your shadow. Like my sister's dog, Sweet Thing, when you need help all you must do is cry out. God will hear your call and release his power through you.

You must never forget that the enemy doesn't fear *you*, he fears your God. The moment you call on God, the evil one will flee and your spirit will be energized. The God who is present waits for you to trust in him rather than yourself. The warrior within you is awakened by the Lord of Hosts and energized by the God of creation.

Of course, you can know this and still never become a mighty man. To get to that point, another faith builder is necessary.

FAITH BUILDER #3: SPIRITUAL DISCIPLINES

Recently, I watched an interview with Colonel Ted Martin, division commander of the 4th Infantry Division—proudly called the Buffalo Soldiers. For weeks our nation's most powerful fighting force waited in ships off the coast of Turkey while war raged in Iraq.

"Are your troops ready?" Geraldo Rivera asked. "Or did they get rusty on the ships?"

"No sir. We used the time to train."

"Are your tanks ready for the desert?"

"Yes sir. We spent a month in the desert in the United States. We traveled five hundred miles in the sand to prepare ourselves for what we would face here. We're the best

trained, best equipped, and most disciplined fighting force in the world."

As Geraldo wrapped up the interview, I couldn't help but admire the preparation and training endured by the members of the 4th Infantry Division and other United States military forces. Their discipline paid off. Our military and its allies liberated the Iraqi people from Saddam Hussein's reign in less than a month.

Those of us engaged in the war for our heart must exercise spiritual discipline. We must prepare ourselves for spiritual combat as though our life depended on it. Because it does!

Throughout this chapter I've stressed the importance of our identity in Christ. He is the source of our life and power. He alone transforms us into his likeness by grace. Yet, while grace is the means by which God changes us, we must prepare our hearts for his grace to be released.

> **We must prepare ourselves for spiritual combat as though our life depended on it. Because it does!**

The apostle Paul said, "Those who live only to satisfy their own sinful desires will harvest the consequences of decay and death. But those who live to please the Spirit will harvest everlasting life from the Spirit" (Galatians 6:8, NLT). In his book *Celebration of Discipline,* Richard J. Foster points out that a farmer is helpless to grow grain. He can provide the right conditions for the growing of grain. He can plow the ground, plant the seed, and water the ground, but then all he can do is allow the natural forces of the earth to take over. After a

few weeks, the life in the seed germinates and up comes a plant.

Similarly, the spiritual disciplines *do not* produce spiritual growth. They are "God's way of getting us into the ground; they put us where he can work within us and transform us."[2] They are the environment where the grace of God can produce the life of Christ in us.

Just as a soldier must prepare for battle through a rigorous training routine, so we must prepare for battle by disciplining ourselves spiritually. I've never known a man who grew spiritually who did not consistently practice spiritual disciplines. As I encourage men to strengthen the warrior within I suggest they make four spiritual disciplines a part of their daily routine.

1. **Read the Bible.** If you aren't in this habit, start small, perhaps with a chapter a day. If you find a verse that is especially relevant, commit it to memory. Before you read, take a moment and ask God to use his Word to show you a single area of your life that needs to be changed. Ask him to speak to you. As you read, answer two questions: 1) What does this passage mean? 2) How does it apply to my life today?

2. **Pray.** I encourage men to buy a journal and write their personal goals. I identify my spiritual, physical, relational, and professional goals on an annual basis. It helps to review them daily and bring them before God. I've found that if I pray at night without a journal my mind wanders and I lose focus. Or else I go into deep

meditation and don't come out of it until the next morning. A journal helps me stay focused and enables me to recall God's faithfulness. You can enter the names of family members and close friends and jot down a request by each name along with the date. As your prayers are answered, keep a record of what God has done.

3. **Express love to your family.** Take time each day to tell your wife and kids you love them. If you're single, make a habit of expressing appreciation to family, friends, and fellow employees. Even though my sons no longer live at home, I try to talk with them daily. Every day I celebrate the beauty of my wife and tell her how much I love her. I recently asked Cindy if she tires of my expressions of love and appreciation. Her response was immediate: "No way!"

4. **Maintain sexual purity.** Begin each day with a fresh commitment not to let your eyes look for or linger on an erotic image. If you're married, focus your thoughts on your wife. Dwell on images that you know would please God. Remember, you alone control your eyes; they are the primary gate through which impurity enters your heart.

If these habits aren't a part of your life, I encourage you to start small—perhaps with three to five minutes of Bible reading and prayer. You can gradually build up to longer times. Occasionally someone will ask me why I encourage men only to spend such a small amount of time in these disciplines.

It's not that I want them to *only* spend that amount of time. Rather, I want them to set achievable goals.

Suppose an out-of-shape and overweight man approached a personal trainer and said, "I want to get in shape." He showed the trainer a picture of what he wanted his body to look like—washboard abs, steel pecs, and biceps like giant hogs wrestling in sausage casings.

Would the personal trainer tell him, "Tomorrow I want you to run seven miles and work out with weights for an hour"? Of course not! He would provide the client with a light workout. Over time the exercise routine would expand. If the man faithfully followed the regimen, his body would begin to resemble the picture.

Similarly, if you want to look like Jesus, you must work out. You must discipline yourself. If you want to grow spiritually, commit to a regimen of daily spiritual disciplines you know you can keep. Psychologists have learned that after someone has done something for twenty-one consecutive days it's a habit. Once you've developed a habit you can expand on it.

I like to remind men that even a small change in their behavior will radically transform their life. Suppose a plane departs from London heading for Seattle, Washington. If the pilot makes a one percent change in the trajectory of the plane, it will end up in Portland, Oregon—a very different destination than the pilot had planned. Similarly, a small change in the trajectory of your life will put you in a dramatically better place in one year.

There is another reason I urge you to start with a spiri-

tual routine you know you can keep. As you meet with God each day, you will experience his presence and power in a fresh way. As the psalmist said, you will "taste and see that the Lord is good" (Psalm 34:8). As you experience the goodness of God, you will desire to spend more time with him. You will crave his Word and celebrate the way he uses it to change your life. If you set your initial goals too high, you'll become discouraged because you can't consistently meet them. Or you'll be so focused on checking things off your list that you may not have time to simply enjoy being in God's presence.

SAINT CRISPIN'S DAY

An excerpt from Shakespeare's play *Henry V* can be a dramatic motivation as we seek to be transformed from passive men to mighty men. Driven to lay claim to the French crown and win back cities in France that had once belonged to England, Henry V leads his footmen across northwestern France, seizing one city after another. Although the English are victorious, the price is high. Aware of the weakening condition of Henry's troops, brought on by dysentery, and their distance from England, the French successfully block Henry's move to a port from which he hopes to return home.

When the English consider the overwhelming force of the heavily armored, highly skilled French knights, their morale plummets. As the two armies prepare for battle at Agincourt, King Henry V, played by Kenneth Branagh in the 1989 movie version, overhears his cousin, Westmoreland,

say, "O that we now had here but one ten thousand of those men in England that do no work to-day!"

A moment later the king delivers to his army the most inspirational call to arms ever penned. The words of Shakespeare, written almost two hundred years after the battle of Agincourt (1415), remain a dramatic expression of what godly leadership meant in the Middle Ages.

> "If we are mark'd to die, we are enow [enough]
> To do our country loss; but if to live,
> The fewer men, the greater the share of honour. . . .
> We few, we happy few, we band of brothers;
> For he to-day that sheds his blood with me
> Shall be my brother; be he ne'er so vile,
> This day shall gentle his condition: [make him
>   a member of the gentry, even if he is a
>   commoner]
> And gentlemen in England now-a-bed [sleeping]
> Shall think themselves accursed they were not
>   here,
> And hold their manhoods cheap whiles any speaks
> That fought with us upon Saint Crispin's day. . . .
> All things are ready, if our minds be so.*[3]

After the king's inspirational speech, every man in the army has a focused mind and feels he could defeat the enemy

---

*I've included only portions of Henry's speech for the sake of brevity. If you would like to read the entire speech, find a copy of Shakespeare's *Henry V* or type "St. Crispin's Day speech" into a search engine on the Internet.

alone. A vicious battle ensues, and King Henry fights from the front, wildly swinging his sword. The English swordsmen are vastly outnumbered and face the enemy from all directions, but they fight on. When the battle finally ends and the bodies are counted, the British have prevailed.

While watching the film for the first time I wept at the words of King Henry. I sensed that today, as then, God is looking for a few men who find honor in battle . . . a few men who will lock arms with their brothers and fight the good fight. Men who daily battle for:

- their identity
- personal holiness
- their family
- endurance through pain
- their friends
- a strong faith

God is looking for men who engage in such battles because they know they're involved in the great angelic conflict. They're convinced that nothing else matters when compared to knowing God and fighting at his side.

Do you want to be one of those mighty men? I hope you do. If so, enlist right now to fight in the six battles and discover firsthand how God can transform you and use you to strengthen your family and other men. The battle is raging as you read these words. . . . Grab your sword and enter the fight.

Discussion Questions

1. How does your identity in Christ affect the way you wage spiritual warfare?

2. How does Superman's battle against Rocky illustrate your battle against Satan and your flesh?

3. Why did most men in ancient Israel fail to live as great warriors (Leviticus 26:7-8)?

4. Read 2 Kings 6:15-17. How would such a vision change the way you wage spiritual warfare?

5. How does a conscious awareness of the power and presence of God help you win the battle for your heart?

6. What must you do to tap into the power of God? How must you think and act?

7. Why are the spiritual disciplines so important in the battle for your heart?

8. What steps will you take to strengthen yourself spiritually?

JOIN THE MOVEMENT

After reading the story of David's mighty men, I sensed God calling me to encourage guys to become modern-day mighty men. I launched a ministry called Million Mighty Men with the belief that revival would come, one man and one day at a time. My vision is for a million men to say: "I want to daily engage in the six battles of a mighty man, and I want to lock arms with others who share my desire for spiritual victory."

In order to engage as warriors in the great angelic conflict, I ask men to agree to practice the daily disciplines mentioned at the end of the previous chapter. I realize that these disciplines aren't the end-all in spiritual warfare. However, they equip us to fight the six battles by enabling us to deepen our relationship with God and our family.

As we engage the enemy, we'll want to encourage other men to join our ranks and aggressively support their pastor and church.

I would like to invite you to lock arms with me and other men around the world. You can do this by going to *www.sixbattles.com* and entering your name. You'll receive a weekly e-mail from me and become part of a movement of men who have decided we will be bullied no more. By God's grace we will win the battle for our heart and those of our family.

You might also want to encourage your wife to go to *www.millionprayingwomen.com* and sign up for a weekly prayer e-mail that focuses on the needs of men. Revival will not

come without a concentrated prayer effort. As we enter in these six battles we need the focused prayers of our wife and the wives of other mighty men.

If you want more information regarding hosting a *Six Battles Every Man Must Win* event in your church or community, please contact me at: bill@sixbattles.com or at P.O. Box 415, Marylhurst, OR 97036.

ENDNOTES

Chapter Two: The Great Angelic Conflict

[1] Charles R. Swindoll, *Improving Your Serve* (Nashville: W Publishing Group, 1981), 2.

[2] In Genesis 1:28 God is addressing men and women. Both were called to exercise responsible dominion over creation, and both entered the great angelic conflict as combatants. However, the focus of this book is on Adam's responsibility.

Chapter Three: Stand Your Ground: Winning the War for Your Heart

[1] Barna Research Online, "Women Are the Backbone of the Christian Congregations in America," 6 March 2000.

[2] I want to thank Dan Schaeffer for his currently unpublished research and insight into the male context.

[3] Lynn H. Colwell, "Weekend Warriors," Entrepreneur.com, 30 January 2003.

[4] Timothy Egan, "Wall Street Meets Pornography," *New York Times,* 23 October 2000.

[5] Ibid.

[6] Mark R. Laaser, "The Pornography Trap," *New Man,* September-October 2002, ix.

Chapter Four: Battle One: Fight for Your Identity

[1] The name Josheb-Basshebeth is found in the Masoretic Text, but the Septuagint has Ishbosheth, presumably from Ishboshet (man of shame). The meaning of the name Josheb-Basshebeth is incomprehensible: "the one dwelling in the

dwelling place." I have concluded the accurate name is "Man of Shame" and for the sake of brevity call him "Shame."

Chapter Five: Battle Two: Fight for Personal Holiness

[1] R.C. Sproul, *The Holiness of God* (Carol Stream, Ill.: Tyndale House Publishers, 1998), 38.

[2] *Random House Webster's College Dictionary* (New York: Random House, 1997), 1365.

Chapter Six: Battle Three: Fight for Your Family

[1] Barna Research Online, "Born Again Adults Less Likely to Cohabit, Just as Likely to Divorce," 6 August 2001, 2.

[2] Oliver Sacks, *The Man Who Mistook His Wife for a Hat* (New York: Harper & Row, 1987), 11.

[3] Colin Brown, ed., *New International Dictionary of New Testament Theology,* vol. 1 (Grand Rapids, Mich.: Zondervan, 1975), 206.

[4] Abraham, Isaac, and Jacob transferred a blessing given by divine direction. It was certain and specific. Because we lack such absolute divine direction, the blessings we give our children don't guarantee such things as future wealth or many children. But they do guarantee a sense of security and destiny.

Chapter Seven: Battle Four: Fight through Pain

[1] Sam Keen, *Fire in the Belly* (New York: Bantam Books, 1991), 103.

[2] William Shakespeare, *Julius Caesar,* Act 4, Scene 3, lines 217–223.

[3] Patrick Morley, *Man in the Mirror* (Grand Rapids, Mich.: Zondervan, 1997), 68.

[4] Bill Perkins, *When Good Men Are Tempted* (Grand Rapids, Mich.: Zondervan, 1997), 128–132.

Chapter Eight: Battle Five: Fight for Your Friends

[1] M. Scott Peck, M.D., *The Road Less Traveled* (New York: Simon and Schuster, 1978), 108–109.

[2] Herb Goldberg, *The Hazards of Being Male* (New York: New American Library, 1976), 133.

[3] Bill Perkins, *When Good Men Are Tempted,* 150–154.

[4] Ibid., 136–137.

[5] Michael Elliott, "Deadly Mission," *Time,* 18 March 2002.

Chapter Nine: Battle Six: Fight for a Strong Faith

[1] Hugh Ross, *Beyond the Cosmos* (Colorado Springs, Colo.: NavPress, 1996), 89–99.

[2] Richard J. Foster, *Celebration of Discipline* (New York: HarperCollins, 1988), 7.

[3] William Shakespeare, *Henry V,* Act 4, Scene 3, lines 23–25, 63–70, 74.

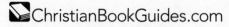ChristianBookGuides.com

Visit www.christianbookguides.com for
a discussion guide and other book-group resources
for Six Battles Every Man Must Win

OTHER BOOKS BY BILL PERKINS

When Good Men Are Tempted

Awaken the Leader Within

The Leadership Bible (contributor)

Available at your local Christian bookstore